OTHER BOARD GAME DESIGN BOOKS
BY JOE SLACK

THE BOARD GAME DESIGNER'S GUIDE TO GETTING PUBLISHED

THE TOP 10 MISTAKES NEW BOARD GAME DESIGNERS MAKE (AND HOW TO AVOID THEM)

THE BOARD GAME DESIGNER'S GUIDE TO CAREERS IN THE INDUSTRY

TABLE OF CONTENTS

SECTION 5 HOW TO TURN A GOOD GAME INTO AN AMAZING GAME

SECTION 6 FINISHING YOUR GAME (HOW TO KNOW IT'S DONE)

SECTION 7 NOW THAT YOUR GAME IS DONE (WHAT'S NEXT?)

RESOURCES

DEDICATION

To my wonderful, amazingly supportive wife, Lisa, and my awesome son, Evan. Thanks for always standing behind me and my dreams!

This is also for all the board game enthusiasts helping to spread the word about our amazing hobby, especially those who are brave enough to try creating their own game.

FOREWORD

My only regret after reading *The Board Game Designer's Guide* is that time travel doesn't exist, because I would very much like to send this book back to myself in 1989.

When I was 8 years old, I had my first desire to design a board game. At the time, I had played a small number of classic games like *Mille Bornes*, *Labyrinth*, *Chess*, and *Monopoly*. I took what I liked about those games and combined them with my youthful love of knights and castles, and the result was a game called *Medieval Quest*. I spent hours brainstorming ideas, illustrating the board, typing out the rules...and I played it exactly once.

Medieval Quest spent the next 22 years in my parents' attic, along with other games I designed during that time. In 2011, I found them during a trip home, and they were part of the catalyst for me to start designing Viticulture. Even then, after years of light game design and participating in the game hobby, I had so much to learn.

Without a doubt, if I had read Joe's book back in 1989, it would have accelerated my progress and potential as a game designer by decades. I would have known from an early age to play a wide variety of games and even look for inspiration beyond the world of games. I would have known to target a specific player experience and use constraints to inspire meaningful decisions through multiple playtests. And I would have known to identify the "golden moment" and accentuate the resulting wow factor to make my games stand out from others on the market.

I've now designed and published several games (*Viticulture*, *Euphoria*, *Scythe*, and *Charterstone*) and developed games by other designers that my company, Stonemaier Games, has published or will publish. Even with that experience, I'm constantly learning, and I found *The Board Game Designer's Guide* to be insightful and inspiring. I hope it has the same impact on you.

Jamey Stegmaier

November 17, 2017

WHAT'S NEW IN THIS EDITION

Don't you hate it when you pick up a new edition of a book and discover that the only changes are a couple of re-worded paragraphs and re-ordered chapters?

Well, that's not what you'll find here. In my opinion, it's not worth creating a new edition unless you have a significant amount of changes or updates, including new information or techniques you've picked up from the time that the original was printed.

Since I published the *Board Game Designer's Guide I have had 6 of my games and expansions published, including 2 that I successfully Kickstarted, both of which funded well over 600%. I've got lots more games on the way as well.*

I've attended conventions, taught game design and development at the University level, released 3 more game design books, and launched 3 of my own courses related to board game design (boardgamedesigncourse.com). I've learned a lot over the last 5 years and I wanted to share my experiences with you.

Throughout this edition, I have updated the information and techniques I use to design and develop games. I've added my top 5 ways to know your game is ready to pitch or publish and an entirely new section with a whopping 13 brand new chapters that dive deeper into game design and turning a good game into an amazing game (which in my mind is critical with the rising amount of competition).

I have also updated and expanded the list of potential publishers you can reach out to pitch your games to, more than doubling the publisher count.

This second edition has over 33% more content. Whether you own the original book or are just jumping in now, you'll find a wealth of information to help you move your game forward fast!

INTRODUCTION

Congratulations! You've taken an amazing first step towards creating your very own board game.

Making a board game seems so easy, but if you've ever tried to design one yourself, you quickly find out there's a lot more involved than you bargained for. Mechanics. Theme. Playtesting. More playtesting. It's enough to make your head spin.

A lot of work goes into something that seems so simple. You have a great idea for a game and it plays perfectly in your head, but when you get it to the table, it falls apart. Or maybe you just can't get past the idea phase.

The good news is, there's a mountain of information out there on how to make a board game. The bad news is, there's a mountain of information out there on how to make a board game.

When I was creating my first game, *Cunning Linguistics*, I was able to find bits and pieces of helpful information, but the problem was, I couldn't find any kind of step-by-step process that would take my idea from start to finish. After having to learn everything by myself the hard way, I wanted to help others interested in getting into board game design so that they could create better games faster, and without all the headaches, wasted money, and missteps that I made.

Creating and publishing a really polished board game doesn't have to be so hard. In this book, I will show you how to take an idea and turn it into an amazing game that people will love. I'm going to walk you through the process step-by-step, first taking your idea and getting it to the table, then playtesting it and making quick iterations, getting it to a final stage, and then helping you figure out what the next best move is for you.

Each chapter of *The Board Game Designer's Guide* will provide you with actionable items, not boring theory. It is a practical guide that will take you from generating an idea to creating a great board game that people (and not just your grandma!) will love. This will allow you to get your game finished quickly, without sacrificing game play and appearance, so that you can get it published and move on to making your next amazing game!

I have played board games my whole life. Everything from *Monopoly*, *Life*, and *Risk*, as a kid, to card games and party games like *Cranium* and *Cards Against Humanity*, classics including *Catan* and *Carcassonne*, and more modern board games such as *Azul* and *Pandemic Legacy*.

In January 2014, on my wife's birthday, while playing a party game with friends for the umpteenth time, I realized that some of the games that we had been focused on had very little replayability, and lost their appeal or shock value after a short time. That's when I decided to create my first game (not counting all the *D&D* adventures I created when I was younger!). I still remember that exact day when it all started.

Since that time, I've created dozens of other games. I now have 6 published games and expansions, through licensing games to other publishers and running my own successful Kickstarter campaigns.

I discovered that I love designing board games just as much (or maybe even more!) than I love playing them. And I **really** love playing them! I'm even a member of the Game Artisans of Canada, which is a small group of really dedicated and incredible (at least in my opinion) board game designers.

When I'm into something, I research the heck out of it. I read every book and blog, and watch every video that I can, then I spend much more time practicing what I've learned (theory can only get you so far, you have to actually do it!). In fact, applying this to Texas Hold'em, and playing hundreds, if not thousands of hours of poker, led me to winning a $3,300 entry into the World Poker Tour Canadian Spring Championship in 2013. This is the exact same approach I have taken with board game design.

I also have a BA in Math and Statistics, with over 17 years of experience in data and analytics, which has been really helpful in my game design. This has been beneficial in understanding probability, randomness, balance, and scoring, among other things, when creating games or helping others to complete their game.

I have taught students about game design and development at University, elementary schools, and board game design camps. I've also hosted and attended more conventions, Protospiels, game design nights and playtesting sessions than I can count. I'm always learning from others and applying what I know to help game designers make their good games great. I've helped aspiring game designers get their ideas out, given them advice and feedback on playtesting, as well as shared my knowledge about publishing, crowdfunding, and all things board game design.

Ever since my first board game idea, I've set out to learn everything there is to know about the process of board game design; every aspect, from prototyping to playtesting to crowdfunding to publishing to trademarking and everything in between. I've learned a ton of lessons and have also made many mistakes along the way. I spent way too much time trying to perfect my games and wasted money where I really didn't need to. I don't want you to make the same mistakes.

I love creating board games. I love seeing other game designers' games come together. I love teaching and helping others. That's why I wrote this book. To help you take your idea and turn it into an amazing game.

If you've got an idea for a game, but just can't get it out of your head, this book will help you take that concept and get it to the table, then take you step-by-step through the process to get your game finished.

Perhaps you've been working on a game and are stuck at some step in the process. Maybe it's the playtesting stage. Maybe your game's just not working, and you don't know what to do or you're not sure about the next step. This book will help you move forward so that you get your amazing game to a completed stage.

If you're working on a game and it's good, but just isn't quite at the level of other games on the market, you'll want to read this book. It will help you get your game finished, and have people beating down your door to play.

Alternatively, if you have a game that's completed, but you just don't know what to do next, this book will help you determine the next step that's right for you. Should you get your game published traditionally? Should you crowdfund or self-publish? Should you create a Print and Play or Print-on-Demand version? Or are you satisfied to just have a good time playing it with friends and family?

The answer is different for every designer. This book will guide you through all the available options so that you can make the best decision for you.

This book will walk you through everything you need to know to create your own board game. Section 1 will walk you through **getting started and generating ideas**. Next, section 2 will get into the **mindset** you'll want to develop in order to be successful and design your game more **efficiently and effectively**. Section 3 is all about the **key elements and considerations** you'll want to have in place to be successful. Then in section 4, we'll get right to the heart of **board game design and playtesting**. This is followed by section 5, a brand new and very detailed section about how to **turn a good game into an amazing game**. Next up is section 6, in which **you'll finish your game** (and understand when it's done). Finally, section 7 will dive into all the options you have available now that your **game is done** and **help you make a definitive decision about what method is best for you**.

Using the simple 4 step process I've learned has allowed me to create a game in months, not years. It can do the same for you. All while saving you a ton of money and headaches as well.

I promise that if you read this book, and follow all the steps outlined, you'll no longer have that idea just stuck in your head. You'll take that concept, quickly create a very rough prototype, and continue to make your game better at every step of the process, until you have a great finished product that you'll be proud of.

If you're willing to put in the time and effort, and follow these same steps that professional game designers follow, your game will be completed so much faster and stand a much better chance of being successful than if you try to figure out all the steps on your own as I had to.

Don't take two years to get your first game finished like I did. Don't waste hundreds or even thousands of dollars, doing the wrong things at the wrong time like I did.

Once you've run through this process for your first game, every one after this will come that much easier. Trust me, once you get the board game design bug, you'll want to keep creating many more games.

It's time to take action. Instead of just thinking about your game, let's start making it!

The board game design process you're about to learn has been used countless times by countless designers to create the world's best board games, many of which I'm sure you've enjoyed yourself. Follow this same process that professional board game designers use, and you'll have your game completed, with gamers demanding to know where they can buy it, in no time.

The process of creating a board game can, and should be, a whole lot of fun. I can't wait to see your game on the shelf. Let's get started!

SECTION 1

GETTING STARTED
AND GENERATING IDEAS

CHAPTER 1
WHY YOU NEED TO DESIGN A BOARD GAME

"We don't stop playing because we grow old; We grow old because we stop playing."

– George Bernard Shaw

So you want to create a board game. That's fantastic! There's probably never been a better time to be a board game designer. Board games are going through a Renaissance period, or some say, a second Renaissance.

More board games are being published and more people are playing them than ever before. Conventions are seeing record attendance numbers. People can't keep up with all the new games on Kickstarter.

While all this is great for the hobby, there's also way more competition. However, you can't deny that it's definitely a lot easier to create a board game and get it out to potential fans than ever.

I know you're eager to get started making your own game, and I don't blame you. Designing board games is amazing! I've been doing this for years and never get tired of working on a new one. Before we start creating, I want to be sure to provide you with the right foundation. By first understanding everything that goes into designing a game, you'll be setting yourself up for success!

In this chapter we'll explore the how's and why's of board game design, get you thinking about the end goal for your game, and introduce you to some common terms you'll want to get acquainted with.

WHY I WROTE THIS BOOK

It was a night I won't forget. I had just gotten home from work and the phone rang. It was my mom. But her voice was different. I could tell right away that something wasn't right. She had just been in a severe car accident. Another driver veered into her lane and hit her head-on.

I went to see her the next morning. She was in a neck brace and in a lot of pain. She was facing a long recovery, but at least she was ok. She was fortunate to have survived.

This really shook me up. It made me realize that life is too short and that anything can happen at any time.

I made a lot of mistakes with my first game and wanted to write this book to help other aspiring game designers like you, but I was hesitant. Two days after the accident I signed up for Self-Publishing School. This course taught me how to quickly write and launch this book, which had been in my head for months.

My mom's accident moved me to action, pushing me to share what I had learned with others right now rather than continue to just think about it. I want to help you and I don't want to have any regrets about not getting this message out.

That's why I wrote this book. To help you make your own board game without making the same mistakes or wasting the time and money that I did.

WHAT DO YOU WANT TO GET OUT OF THIS EXPERIENCE?

Are you a person with a board game idea? Or do you want to become a board game designer? The two are very different. It's easy to come up with a board game idea, or any idea for a product or service for that matter, but it takes a lot more to put that idea into action.

While it may seem easy to create a board game, if you want it to be something that people will really enjoy and keep coming back to, you do have to put in some hard work to get there. Sure, it's fun work, but it's still work.

You're obviously interested in designing a board game since you picked up this book. And I have confidence in you that you're willing to put in the effort to take your idea and develop it into a finished, really enjoyable game. So I have to ask you, why do you want to design a board game? What do you want to get out of this experience?

Are you creating a new game for the fun of it?

Are you designing it for the challenge?

Are you getting into board game design to make money?

Are you looking at this as a possible new career?

Or do you just love the hobby and want to get more involved in the board game community?

All of these are possibilities, although I'll tell you up front that it can be a real challenge to make any significant money from designing board games full-time. So above all, you really have to love board games, along with the whole process of board game design.

There's a lot of fun and a sense of accomplishment that can come from identifying and solving problems for the challenges that come with board game design. I'm a problem-solver myself, so this is another aspect that really appeals to me. Also, if you want to be a successful board game designer, you'll definitely want to get really involved in the board game community.

Just to be clear, when I say board games, I'm really talking about all varieties of tabletop games, including board games, card games, dice games, deduction games, etc. To keep things simple, I'll be using the common term "board games" throughout this book, even for those games where no board exists.

COMMON TERMS

Since you're diving right into the world of game design, you'll want to be familiar with a number of terms that are used within the board game community. I've collected a number of these common terms along with a number of different game types for your reference in the glossary at the back of this book.

WHAT GOAL DO YOU HAVE IN MIND FOR YOUR GAME?

While I really want you to focus on the design of your game and taking it from concept to a complete, really enjoyable experience, I also want you to keep your end goal in mind. Although this may change over the course of designing your game as you learn more about the process and the industry, it's a good idea to know what you want to do with your game once it's finished.

This is even more relevant if you're working with a co-designer. If you have different goals for your game when it's completed, and can't come to an agreement, it may never see the light of day.

I'm going to talk briefly about some of the options you have when your game is completed. I'll go into more details about each of these options in section 6, but for now I want to give you an introduction so that you'll have an idea of what you'd like to do with your game once it's done.

ARE YOU LOOKING TO GET YOUR GAME PUBLISHED BY AN ESTABLISHED GAME PUBLISHER?

This is definitely a good option if you want to focus on game design and are not interested in all the business aspects that go along with game publishing. While there is a lot of competition, if you can design a game that fits well with the publisher's catalogue, you could see your game on the shelf of major stores across the world.

While this may not make you rich, 5% of something is much better than one hundred percent of nothing. Now, the royalties you earn on a game may vary, so this is just an example. Remember that going this route also lets you focus on game design and moving on to your next game rather than splitting your time between game design and business.

WHAT ABOUT KICKSTARTER OR ANOTHER CROWDFUNDING SITE?

There are a number of crowdfunding sites online, but since Kickstarter has really shown itself to be the go-to place for board games, we'll focus our attention here.

If you're familiar with Kickstarter, you've no doubt seen some of the huge success stories. Tabletop games generally do fairly well on this platform, and there have even been some games that have made millions of dollars here (or have gone on to make millions). However, there are a few things they don't tell you.

For example, while board games have a relatively high success rate that is well over 50%, many of the goals are very low and are just barely met. You might have a successful campaign, however, you may only bring in $5,000-$10,000 in revenue. Remember as well that this is revenue, not profit – you still have to deliver a game to all your backers.

This amount may not even be enough to cover your first print run. Moreover, while there is minimal risk, at least up until you meet your funding goal, if you don't budget well, or take into account any of the possible problems that could arise, you could actually lose money on the project. It's easy to highlight the big successes, but in reality, 1% of board game campaigns are bringing in nearly half of all the money.

And why do the successful campaigns make so much money? It's usually because the creator is well known, and the project has some really phenomenal marketing behind it. If nobody knows who you are, and you haven't been promoting this game heavily leading up to your launch, you're unlikely to be very successful.

Oh, and all the stats I've mentioned above? They're based on projects that were completed. Canceled projects are not included in these numbers. So the success rate is also inflated.

Did I mention that if you run a Kickstarter campaign and are successful, you'll now be running your own business? You'll have to take on all the responsibilities, and will have to figure out shipping, manufacturing, fulfillment, marketing, and all the other things that go along with being a board game publisher.

You must be good at budgeting and considering all possible contingencies, because if you miss one thing, your once-profitable project will now be losing money. You're taking on all the risk, but also getting all the rewards.

Everyone I've talked to who has run a Kickstarter campaign has said it was a **lot** more work than he or she ever expected. Oh, and you probably also have a day job, right? These are just a few of the things you want to keep in mind.

WHAT ABOUT OTHER OPTIONS?

You can always self-publish. If you run a crowdfunding campaign, you will essentially be doing this as well, but you can also decide to start completely on your own.

This route is definitely full of risks. You're investing your own capital to get the games made, and unless you use a fulfillment system, you will be storing and shipping them all yourself. Between the investment and work involved, this can be a daunting task. It has been done and there are some success stories, but you'll want to make sure there is a serious demand for your game before you consider this option.

You can also make your game a Print and Play (PnP) file. This is by far the easiest thing to do, as you'll likely just be uploading a PDF on your own website or another board game site for people to download, then print and play (as the name suggests).

This can be done as a free PDF or you could charge customers for the game, however very few gamers are interested in doing all this work themselves, so they're even less likely to pay for a PnP. This can however work very well for playtesting, especially if you don't have a great number of playtesters in your area to try out your game.

You can also use Print-on-Demand services such as the Gamecrafter. Using this method, there are no minimum print runs, instead you upload all your files, component lists, rules, etc. to the site, and people can pay to get a copy of your game. This is printed as a one-off and will be shipped directly to their door. While this is much easier and less costly for you, the cost of the games can be a lot more for the buyer. Not everybody is familiar with this option, so it can be harder for others to find your game.

You could also be creating this game simply for fun. There's nothing wrong with that. If you, your friends, and your family have a great time playing your game, that can be its own reward.

CREATING MORE GAMES

If you're anything like me, once you've finished your first game you will have caught the board game design bug and just want to keep creating more and more games. You may have ideas coming fast and furious and can't wait to try out your next game concept.

This is a great place to be. You have the confidence knowing you've already created one game that people really enjoy, and you'll want to keep developing more board games and new experiences for those around you.

This is just a brief introduction to the possibilities that await you once you've finished your first game. You may have an idea in mind right now for what you want to do with your game when it's completed, but note that this may change by the time your game is done. That's okay. You can always change your mind.

If you keep creating more great games, you may want to stick with one route, or you may want to try multiple methods to see what works best for you. It's really your decision. No one is saying you have to stick with one option. Just keep creating more amazing games and spreading our awesome hobby with the rest of the world!

THE DISTINCTION BETWEEN A BOARD GAME DESIGNER AND A BOARD GAME DEVELOPER

You may see the terms "board game designer" and "board game developer" used interchangeably in the board game world, however they are two distinct and important roles in the creation of most good board games.

While the definition of each is not completely agreed upon within the community, board game design tends to focus more around the person who came up with the original idea, produced and tested early versions of the game, and moved this forward to a nearly finished stage for publishing.

A developer on the other hand, typically is employed by a publisher. They will take this game from the designer and continue to refine it until the publisher feels it is ready to be released.

There definitely can be overlap between these two roles, as both perform a lot of playtesting, tweaking, and improving the game. In the case of a small self-publisher, it could be the same person in charge of both the design and the development work. A board game designer intending to self-publish may also hire a board game developer to help take his or her game to the next level and improve the chances of success.

DESIGNING SOLO OR WITH A PARTNER (OR PARTNERS)

As with just about everything, there are pros and cons to whatever approach you take. If you make your game all by yourself, this allows you more flexibility, control, and the ability to work on this whenever you have the time.

Having a partner on the other hand, will help keep you accountable and split the workload (which is especially helpful if each of you has different skills that will help make the game even better). But this will also mean splitting the rewards.

So, what's the best approach? That's really up to you.

Just because you create your first game on your own, doesn't mean you can't collaborate with somebody in the future, or vice versa. You can always try out both approaches, and you may have to work on different games with different people before you find a good match.

Whatever you decide, always keep in mind that it takes many people to make a great game. You may be the designer, but you must also rely on playtesters, other designers, and whomever you work with along the way to get your game published, to ensure that your game isn't just good, but the best it can be. It really does take a community to make an amazing board game.

So, with all this talk about board games, I bet you're itching to play one. Let's get right to it in the next chapter!

ACTION: First, familiarize yourself with the common board game terms and list of mechanics. You don't have to memorize them all right now. You can always refer back to them.

Now, decide on the approach and end goal you want to take with your current game. Do you plan to pitch this to a publisher? Or are you going the self-publishing route, either directly, or by starting with Kickstarter or another crowdfunding platform? Will you make this game available via Print and Play or through a Print-on-Demand service? Or are you just making this for the enjoyment of yourself, your friends, and your family?

CHAPTER 2
PLAY LOTS OF GAMES!

"Just one game,' they said, and started to play – that was yesterday."

– Chinese proverb

As a board game designer, I encourage you to play lots of games. I know, I know. It's a hardship. I'm asking you to do a lot here. But in all seriousness, playing a variety of different games will give you a good feeling for all the varieties of games out there, help you determine the types of games you enjoy playing, and give you lots of ideas for what you can do to improve your game.

PLAY A VARIETY OF GAMES

Think of this as research. By playing a wide variety of games, you'll broaden your knowledge, while having fun at the same time. That's the kind of research that everyone should be lucky enough to do!

If you only play party games, then try a more complex Euro game. If you mostly play Euro games, try a cooperative game. With so many different types of games available, you really need to get a feel for what's out there.

By playing a variety of games, you'll also learn about different mechanics that designers use, both by themselves, and in conjunction with other mechanics. This will give you a good feel for how games work, and how designers introduce challenges and interesting decisions for players.

You'll see mechanics you've never seen before, and applied in ways you've never imagined. You may pick up some mechanics that will work well in your game, or ones you might want to try in future designs. You'll also see which mechanics help or even slow down and hinder a game. With this knowledge, you'll become a better game designer.

You'll also discover what games are popular and get a better understanding of why this is the case. You'll see what types of games appeal to the hard-core hobbyist, the casual gamer, and the mass market. You'll see why people are talking about certain games so much in forums and meet ups, and you'll make your own judgments about whether these games appeal to you.

By playing a wide variety of games, you'll also figure out what types of games you enjoy the most. This is really important to figure out early on, because the games you will be creating are also the games you'll be playing a whole lot. Through the process of designing a game, you'll play your game over and over, in different iterations, and with many people, so you'd better like it!

Here are some suggestions from myself and other designers on games that all designers should try or at least be familiar with:

- *Dungeons & Dragons (D&D)*

- *Magic: The Gathering*

- *Catan*

- *Ticket to Ride*

- *Dominion*

- *Cards Against Humanity* and/or *Apples to Apples*

- *Agricola* and/or *Stone Age*

- *7 Wonders*

- *Dixit* and/or *Codenames*

- *The Resistance*

- *Love Letter*

- *Pandemic* (along with *Pandemic Legacy*)

FIND GAPS IN THE MARKET

By playing a lot of games, you'll see what exists in the market and what untapped areas you might find. There may be a number of unexplored themes that could be interesting ideas for games. It seems that one theme becomes popular and suddenly you see a whole rush of games coming out based on that theme. If you can uncover a new game idea that hasn't been explored, or at least not in as much detail as you would like, there may be a real opportunity there.

There may also be chances to explore completely new genres. For example, games used to typically be competitive, but over time more team games, cooperative games, and one-versus-many games have been introduced. More and more legacy games are also being created. There's always a new idea out there, you just have to discover what that might be.

What audiences or groups are being left out of the board game hobby? What group sizes or dynamics don't have a great representation of games available?

When creating your game, it's important to understand your target audience. Will it appeal to the mass market? Hard-core hobbyists? A specific profession? Or a different group entirely?

Maybe there's an opportunity to design a game to help a particular market or industry. You may have some background knowledge in this area and can apply this to a board game. Maybe there's even a group of people that this board game would help. What about a game for kids with learning disabilities? Autism? The sky's the limit.

You can also get many ideas and learn lessons from other markets. You could look at different entertainment genres such as video games, music, and movies for example.

Video games often have save points, power meters, inventories, different difficulty levels, and end bosses. Many successful games spawn sequels.

DVD movies have chapters, extras, and other features.

Perhaps there are other industries we can learn from and apply some of their great aspects to board games.

GET INVOLVED IN THE BOARD GAME COMMUNITY

Check around your local area to see if there are groups for gamers or board game designers to get together on a regular basis. Do you have board game stores or board game cafés in your community? Perhaps there are restaurants that carry a selection of games for patrons to play, or host game nights.

Maybe there are game night meet-ups at people's homes or community centres. Get out there and see what's happening in your neighbourhood.

This is also a great opportunity to meet other game enthusiasts. By doing this you can widen your knowledge of different games and have the opportunity to play games you've never heard of, or ones you otherwise wouldn't have tried, but may end up actually enjoying. It's really important to branch out beyond the games you normally would play with the people you always play with.

Whether these groups are game designers or, just fans of board games, you may uncover many opportunities to collaborate or brainstorm game ideas with them. If there is a particular type of game you like, others may also point you towards similar games with the suggestion "if you liked that game you might like this one too."

Playing games with others in your community, and talking about your own game ideas, will also allow you to find out if any of your ideas are already being used, and if so, how they are being applied in other board games. Maybe there's a game just like yours already on the market. You can't possibly know every game that's ever been made, or every game mechanic used. But others may have played games that will be of interest to you.

People who are really into the hobby can also give you great suggestions as well. They may recommend an idea that has already been used, where you might want to try a particular spin on it. Maybe they have something in mind that they'd really like to see, but have no interest in creating such a game. This really opens up a lot more conversation and can help you tremendously with your game design.

If you can find other board game designers in your area, one of the best things you can do is show interest and playtest their games. This will not only lead to more ideas for your own games, but will also broaden your experience in the gaming world and give you a chance to give back and help others.

It really does take a community to create a board game, and by helping others, they will most likely be very eager to help you as well. We all want to see more great games on the market and are willing to help each other out to get there.

If you have difficulty finding board game and game designer events, this is a great opportunity to start forming your own groups for playtesting. You can playtest each other's games and let each other know about playtesters who are interested in trying out new games in progress. Over the course of designing your game, you want to playtest with a lot of different people and in a variety of groups, including showing it to a number of different designers, so this step is crucial.

DIFFERENT PERSPECTIVES AND POINTS OF VIEW

Another thing you may notice when you play a variety of games is the use of different perspectives. Instead of just being able to play as the human hero, many games allow you to play on the side of evil, as an animal, or from some other viewpoint you might not expect. For example, what if you were to retell the story of the "*Three Little Pigs*" as a board game in which the player plays the role of the wolf?

You may also get ideas for re-theming a game. Put characters in a different world like a fish-out-of-water scenario. Bring characters out of stories from the past into the future, or vice versa. Take a common theme and place everything underwater, or in space. The possibilities are only limited by your imagination!

Games are also a great opportunity to allow players to take on roles they normally wouldn't dream of. Allow players to take on the role of a villain or monster, instead of the typical knight in shining armour. Have players cast in the role of mob bosses, or some other underworld character.

A great example of this is *Burgle Bros*. This is a cooperative game where all players take on the role of thieves working together to rob a bank. This takes players out of reality and into a fantasy world where they can act out in ways that they would never normally even consider in the real world. This can be really exciting and appealing to a lot of players.

Taking on a different point of view can lead to some really outside the box thinking. A great example of this is *Vast: The Crystal Caverns*. This asymmetrical game allows players to take on a variety of different possible roles. You can even play as the cave! In the role of the cave you to try to swallow the adventurers before they can escape. This is a fantastic example of thinking in a really different way.

What role would you like to take on in a game? What's something you'd never dream of doing in real life, but would like to do vicariously through game role play? Can you design a game where players are a building or inanimate object? Let your mind wander and come up with the craziest, most outrageous ideas, and see if there's something that you can incorporate.

CONTESTS

Keep your eyes open for board game design contests. You'll occasionally see publishers or board game websites announce contests for specific types of games. Maybe one of these will really speak to you and you'll decide to design a game and compete in the contest. This may get your game a lot of attention, or possibly even published!

Now you should have lots of methods of getting ideas for your game. Don't lose them! We're about to get into the best way to snatch those ideas out of thin air and ensure you never forget a concept for a great game.

ACTION: Play at least three games you've never played before, and play at least one of them with a group of people you've never played with. Be open to suggestions from other people or try a game you've never heard of or don't know much about. Think about what is good about the game and what could be improved. By doing this, you'll start to think more and more like a game designer.

CHAPTER 3
WRITE IT DOWN!

"The successful people are the ones who can think up things for the rest of the world to keep busy at."

– Don Marquis, novelist and humourist

Let's dive right into some more suggestions on how to generate tons of ideas and make sure you never lose a single one.

TAKE A NOTEBOOK WHEREVER YOU GO

You never know when a good idea will strike, so you have to be prepared. Take a notebook or some other means to capture your thoughts wherever you go. Remember, the best method is the one you'll use.

I know, you're thinking you'll just jot it down later. The problem is you can't always rely on your memory. So much happens through the course of a day that you'll really want to capture something right at the moment it hits. So make sure you always have some way to seize that idea before it gets away.

I also suggest you jot down **any** idea, no matter how crazy. That crazy idea may not necessarily be the next hit game, but it may lead you into another line of thinking that could produce a really great game idea. It also doesn't matter if it's an incomplete thought. Maybe a partial name, some random concept, or a weird mechanic comes to you unexpectedly. It can't hurt to write it down.

There have been a number of times that I've come up with just a name. I didn't know what the game might actually be about at first, but I liked the name and thought it had the potential to become a game. I've often come back to that idea later, and developed a concept for a game based merely on that title alone.

LOOK FOR INSPIRATION EVERYWHERE

Ideas can come from anywhere. You have to be ready to pluck them from the air wherever you find them.

While board games are typically played indoors, you may find a lot of interesting ideas waiting for you outside, in nature. Animals interacting with each other; the way a tree blows in the wind; or anything else you can imagine.

You can't just sit by your computer or game table and expect great ideas to rush to you. You have to get out and walk around. Do something different. What do you notice? Talk to others, notice people's conversations, and explore the world around you. Be open to any suggestions that come to mind.

An idea can also come to you while you're at work. Maybe something a coworker says, a typo in an email, or an unusual situation.

Ideas can often come when you're watching a movie or show, or even playing a video game. There might be a certain aspect of a scene or level that really appeals to you, and you may think of a way to turn that into an idea for a board game. *Boss Monster* for example, is inspired by old 8-bit video games, in which you play as the end level boss.

I mentioned previously that you should play a lot of board games, and this may help you generate even more ideas for your own game. Consider removing aspects you don't like in a game, and focusing on the really fun part of it. I'm not suggesting that you steal a game idea, but you can certainly borrow aspects from other games and make them your own.

For example, my family used to play a card game called *Frustration* after holiday dinners. It was a lot of fun, but very frustrating at the same time, as the name suggests. One of the problems with that game I always found though was that it often took two to three hours to play. That can feel quite long for a simple card game, especially if you're way behind the other players and don't feel like you have a chance to win.

I wanted to find a way to convey that same experience, but in a much shorter time frame. I ended up converting Frustration into a fast-paced simultaneous dice rolling game, which allowed the game to be played in about 20 minutes, while still giving players a similar feeling to the card game. My version also improved on the game so that all players were always in the race, and there was never a runaway winner.

Quite often I'll hear somebody say something, and I find myself thinking, "Hey, that could be a great idea for a game." For instance, one day when the expression "awesome sauce" came to my mind, I just had to write it down. I figured there had to be a game in there somewhere. I was able to make a really cool chef competition game with an element of sabotage, based solely on that name.

There was another time that I was with my family on vacation at a resort, and they had a couple of workers from a local wildlife reserve come in to show the kids some wild animals and talk about each of them. They mentioned that squirrels bury their nuts in holes, but also dig some holes and fill them back in, in case another squirrel or other animals are watching, to throw them off so that they won't lose their collection.

I thought this would be an interesting concept for a game, so I immediately jotted it down. At the time of this writing, I haven't yet developed anything around this thought, but it is on my list of ideas to come back to later. It's always good to have a list like this to revisit when you're looking for ideas.

WHERE/WHEN DO IDEAS COME TO YOU?

Where do you find inspiration? Make sure to note when and where ideas often come to you. Is it when you're in the shower? Taking a walk? Feeling the sand between your toes at the beach? Your places of inspiration will be different from the next person. What's important is to know where to go and what to do when you want to generate new ideas.

Take the time to daydream, relax, and let your mind wander. Ideas and solutions often come when you least expect them. They will sometimes come at a later time, after you've been thinking about an issue for a little while.

You're less likely to find these inspirations when you're stressed out. You're much better off taking a break and coming back to it with a fresh set of eyes and new perspective. An idea might come to you in between, or maybe when you sit back down to give it another go. And when in doubt, go play a new game!

You now have some great ideas for your game. You should protect them and not talk about them, so nobody will be able to steal them, right? Wrong. This is actually the worst approach you can take. We'll discuss why sharing your idea rather than hiding it will get your game finished sooner, and why it will be so much better as a result in the next chapter.

ACTION: Find or buy a notebook or other device that you know you will use to make notes about game ideas. Whether it's electronic or pen and notebook, it has to be something you will keep with you and actually use. You may want to try a couple different approaches to see what works best for you. Oh, and as you're writing down your ideas, make sure to note when and where inspiration has struck you. These are places you'll want to return to whenever you're stuck or looking for new ideas.

CHAPTER 4
PROTECT YOUR IDEA?

"I have plenty of ideas—hundreds of them. I think most game designers do. The challenge is executing those ideas."

— Jamey Stegmaier, Kickstarter expert and creator of Scythe

In this chapter, we'll talk about when you should and shouldn't protect your idea, how to do so, and the difference between trademarks, copyrights, and patents.

Stop Worrying About Other People Stealing Your Ideas

I know what you're thinking. You've got this great concept for a game that no one has ever thought of. Your concern is that if you tell anyone, even someone you trust, your idea will be stolen. I've been there, and I thought in the exact same way. It took me some time before I was ready to share my idea with others, especially those I didn't know.

But honestly, ideas are a dime a dozen. I used to believe that they were sacred, but now I see them in a different light. Everyone is busy with his or her own ideas, and they don't have time to steal yours. I'm not trying to be harsh, rather trying to help you understand that if you're going to be a successful board game designer, you'll quickly learn that you need help from others.

One of the other things I've learned the hard way, is that nobody is going to be as excited about your idea as you are. People in general tend to gravitate to their own ideas, and most game designers are too busy trying to turn their own ideas into a full-fledged game.

That's not to say that an idea or prototype has never been stolen or work of writing has never been plagiarized. It's always a good idea to document your work and make sure you have timestamps to prove the creation date.

WHAT'S THE BIG IDEA?

It's entirely possible that someone else will come up with a very similar concept to yours, even at the exact same time. There's a term for this. It's known as simultaneous invention.

Let's say you come up with an idea for a board game about hunting. The next thing you know you see a hunting board game on the shelves of your local department store. Did someone steal your idea? A hunting game is a pretty vague concept, and your idea may have been little more than this. Is the gameplay of this new game you spotted exactly the way you had it in your head? Maybe you hadn't thought ahead that far yet.

Until an idea is developed, it's not worth much. The idea needs to be created into something tangible. If you want to be a board game designer, and not just someone with a board game idea, you need to develop this concept by taking action and transforming it into an actual game.

You're going to need help and feedback from others to make your good game great! You're far better off sharing your idea with others, particularly in the form of an early prototype, to find out ways to make your game even better. This will also help you to understand if there are any other similar games on the market, and if you need to make any significant changes or move on to the next idea.

I worked on my first game, *Cunning Linguistics*, mostly by myself and with one trusted friend, and played it with only a small number of people at first. If I could do it all over again I would have played my game with other designers much, much earlier.

Like any inventor, I didn't want to have my idea stolen; I even went so far as to trademark the name of my game. Don't make the same mistakes I did. I wasted $772 on trademarks in Canada and the US for my first game. Add to this the hundreds of dollars I spent on early prototypes, barcodes, shipping, and donations for reviewers (some of which weren't the best match for my game, and depending on my next step may no longer be relevant), and I can (not-so-proudly) say that I wasted well over $1,000 on one game alone. Don't make the same mistakes that I did!

Oh, and to top it all off, the Canadian trademark took a full year to go through, and that was with no problems at all. The US trademark on the other hand, took about two years to get settled. That's a serious delay for releasing a game!

Knowing what I know now, I could have saved myself a ton of time and money. Don't worry about having your idea stolen. You should share your game with others. Scratch that. You **need** to share your game with others!

DIFFERENT TYPES OF PROTECTION

Having said all this, it's really helpful to know what types of protection are available, and which ones are relevant to board game design. Now I'm not a lawyer or trademark expert. I'm just sharing with you what I know about the subject. I definitely suggest you consult a professional and/or do your own research should you decide to pursue any type of protection for your game.

There are a few types of protection, and you want to understand what each means. There are **trademarks, registered trademarks, copyrights**, and **patents**. I'll go over each one of these in a bit more detail here.

Trademark: A trademark can be used to protect a word, design, or sound, and may also include the particular style used (example: The Nike logo and swoosh). Once submitted, there is a limited amount of protection that comes with a trademark, which is enhanced once the process is complete and the trademark is registered. This is the most relevant protection used in the board game industry.

Registered Trademark: Registering your trademark gives you more legal protection than an unregistered trademark. This makes it easier to remedy any infringements.

Copyright: A copyright protects literary, musical, and artistic work. For example, a copyright may be placed on a song or other work of art. You're not likely to use this type of protection for your board game, except perhaps on your website. While anything you write and publish is automatically owned by you, having a copyright on your materials stating this can often dissuade someone who may be thinking about stealing content from you.

Patent: A patent is generally used to protect a new invention or improvement to an existing invention. These are used very infrequently in relation to board games.

REASONS TO CONSIDER A TRADEMARK

As mentioned above, a trademark is the most likely type of protection you would want to use if you choose to protect your board game. Let's explore the reasons you may want to consider a trademark.

You may be thinking about using a trademark to ensure a name you're considering is not already in use. You may also want to avoid trouble or lawsuits down the road. However, there are some simple methods you can use to keep yourself out of trouble.

When it comes to board games, Boardgamegeek is the place to go to find out anything you want related to the board game community. They have an inventory of practically every game ever made, with great search functionality. This is the first place to look to see if there is a name or similar concept already in existence.

The next thing you can do is a simple Google search. See if the name is in use, whether it be for a website, or other product. Even if there is no board game with the same name, you want to make sure there isn't an electronic game or anything else using the same name if possible. You may also want to be able to claim a website domain with this name later on.

Lastly, you can do a trademark registry search. Look up the intellectual property or trademark registry website for your home country (and possibly others) to see if a trademark already exists for the name you're considering.

These three searches are the first places to start. However, if you want to be completely certain, you can always contact a trademark agent to assist you with the search. There will, of course, be costs involved with this, but it will also bring you peace of mind.

Another reason you may be considering a trademark is you're worried someone may steal your name or idea. You must keep in mind that at this point your game is unknown. It would have to become a huge success before this would be a concern. Therefore, it's probably better to wait until such time.

There are some ways to get around these concerns. For example, you can use place names. You can also consider other words and terms that are so common, they couldn't possibly be trademarked. Even if you take one of these approaches, you'll still want to complete the searches above, and do your homework to make sure you won't have problems using that name.

WAIT (BUT WHY?)

Again, you want to consider what the end goal is with your game. If you are even considering pitching to a publisher, then the trademark, or any other type of protection, is completely unnecessary.

Why is that you ask? Well, the publisher will take care of all of this. Besides, once you've signed your game with a publisher, they have the right to change the name, theme, and any other aspect of the game. So, any trademark purchase might be completely wasted. Publishers also see trademarking your game as an amateur move.

If you have a trademark on your game, the publisher may not be interested. Publishers want to work with designers who are easy to get along with. You have to be willing to share your game with them, and let them make the necessary changes to make your game something that people will want to buy.

And don't even consider asking them to sign a nondisclosure agreement in order to protect your rights, because they will just pass on your game. There are so many ideas out there, and they may even have a game in development that is similar to yours. They just can't take the risk that someone is going to come back and sue them in this type of scenario.

TIME AND MONEY

Trademarks can also be very costly. Did you know that every country or region has its own process? It's not only a matter of purchasing one trademark and being covered across the world. If you wanted complete protection, you would need to submit and pay for a trademark in every individual region around the globe. This could end up costing you a lot of money.

Of course, you could hire a trademark agent to do all this for you, at the cost of many tens of thousands of dollars, but you also have to consider the fact that at this point you haven't sold a single game. Is it really worth investing so much money in something before you even know anyone's going to buy it?

Not only is the process costly, it is also extremely time-consuming. The time from submission to completion can often take 12 to 18 months or more. And that's if everything goes smoothly.

If there's another company or product with an even remotely similar name, you might have spent time and money on a trademark application for nothing. Add to this the fact that waiting on a trademark will definitely delay the release of your game and will take away time you could be spending designing games, and you'll realize this may not be the approach you want to take.

Even if you're considering self-publishing, whether doing this directly, or through crowdfunding, you're better off taking a safe name and not worrying about trademarking it, at least until your game is at a high level of popularity and generating enough money to warrant looking into this further.

The next section is all about establishing you with the tools you'll need to be a productive and amazing game designer. Let's get set up!

ACTION: Share your game idea with someone you don't know, or don't know very well. It's even better if this person is another board game designer or avid board game enthusiast. You'll feel better getting this off your chest and you will start opening yourself up to sharing your game idea with others, which is crucial for it to become the best game it can be.

SECTION 2

MINDSET

CHAPTER 5

STAY FOCUSED!

"It is the greatest of all mistakes to do nothing because you can do only a little. Do what you can."

- Sydney Smith, English writer

Now you might be wondering why I'm talking about mindset here. Isn't this a book about designing board games? Of course it is. But in order to be successful in any creative endeavour, or any undertaking for that matter, you need to maintain focus and be in the right mindset.

WORK ON YOUR GAME EVERY DAY

Consistency is the key. You really have to be persistent. By carving out time each day to work on your game and improve it, you'll be setting yourself up with a fantastic habit. Just like anything, practice will make you better.

The first time you got on a bike you probably fell off a lot. The first time you jumped into a pool you couldn't swim. Whether you want to be an Olympic medalist, world-renowned musician, or board game designer, you have to work at it every day. Thank goodness designing board games is a lot of fun!

You have to put in the hard work. You have to be able to focus on what needs to be done next. One trick I've found that keeps me on track is noting down my next step after I'm finished playtesting, or am done working on a game for the moment.

The next step should be tangible and actionable, like "playtest starting with seven cards each rather than five," or "figure out a way to speed up each player's turn," rather than something generic like "work on this game." That way, the next time I sit down to work on it, I don't have to waste time thinking about what needs to be done. I just look at the next step and keep moving ahead.

It doesn't have to be the same aspect of the game every time you embark on it. You can really work on any part, such as brainstorming names, play-testing, trying out a suggested idea, or anything else to move your game forward. You must make sure however, that whatever you're working on is aimed at improving the game, not just wasting time (like spending hours online looking for the perfect icon – yes, I admit I've done this…).

Working on your game every day will give you a real sense of momentum. Comedian Jerry Seinfeld keeps a huge calendar on his wall displaying all the months of the year. Each day that he works on comedy, he marks an "X." Pretty soon he has a running streak of "X's." This gives him further incentive to keep going, because he doesn't want to break that streak. It's a little thing, but a big motivator to him.

Always make sure to dedicate time to game design. Block off time in your calendar every day, with the aim to work on your game when you feel most productive. Sometimes with work, family, and other responsibilities, it's hard to squeeze in this time, so you may just have to fit it in wherever you can. Nevertheless, it's important that you do this.

LEARN FROM MY MISTAKES

My first game, *Cunning Linguistics*, took two years to complete. Two years. That's a long time, but it didn't have to be. Especially since it wasn't at all complex. It was a simple party game. Sure, I worked on my game here and there, but it wasn't a top priority for me early on. I didn't know the first thing about playtesting, or how to make a great player experience, let alone any of the other important aspects of game design. I had no clue what approach to take.

So, I started learning everything I could, one topic at a time. However, I found out later that I was doing things way out of order, and discovered I still had a lot to learn. I wasted so much time trying to figure out things like trademarking, crowdfunding, and getting printing quotes, when I really should have been focusing on creating an amazing game.

However, it didn't turn out all bad in the end. Spending so much time researching and trying to understand the whole board game design process from beginning to end gave me a ton of knowledge. I now know so much more than I did when I first started. As a result, the games I've been creating ever since have come together much more quickly. I'm sharing all this with you now so that you don't have to spend years trying to piece this together like I did.

Not every game idea I have always pans out (this is true of any game designer!), but more often than not, I'm now able to take an idea and turn it into a polished game in a matter of months, not years. I only wish a book like this existed when I was first starting out!

ALWAYS BE MOVING FORWARD

As a game designer, you'll always be testing new ideas. Think of yourself as a scientist. You come up with a hypothesis, such as "my game will play better if players are allowed to do four actions on their turn instead of three."

Then you test this to see if your hypothesis is true. If not, no big deal. Just go back to the previous version or try something new. That's what game design is all about. Test, test, test. Each test will bring you closer to a finished game that people are going to really enjoy.

Try playtesting your game with new people. Ask for feedback on a specific aspect of your game. If the group is willing, see if you can try it one way, then another, then maybe a third way, and so on, until you've figured out the right formula. New people have new ideas, so there'll always be something additional to ponder.

Talk about your game with other people. It could be with friends, board game enthusiasts, or other designers. This will generate more ideas and possible solutions for any challenges you are facing. Don't allow yourself to get stuck. Talk it out. Keep your game moving forward.

Remember that your game is getting closer to completion every day. As long as you keep putting in the time and effort, your game will keep improving, and more and more people will be asking when they can buy a copy. That will definitely keep you motivated to make this effort a priority.

PROCRASTINATION AND DISTRACTIONS

I'll be honest. It can be hard to sit down and work on your game. There are so many things that are easier to do, and most of them require a lot less thought. Working on your game is just that. Work. It's amazing work and can be a lot of fun, but it requires your full attention, which can be hard if you just worked a full day, and then still have to take care of your normal responsibilities.

There will be days you just want to put your feet up and watch TV. That's not to say that you don't need to make time to relax and do the other things you enjoy, but you don't want to start allowing these things to take over your game design time. It's easy to get out of the habit of working on your game if you don't do it consistently.

It's a good idea to set a timer. Decide on a dedicated amount of time you want to work on your game, and commit to working on nothing else during this time. It may be half an hour, an hour, or an afternoon. Maybe you can even squeeze in some time during your lunch break, or jot down some ideas while you're on the bus or train.

Do whatever best suits you. But remember most of the time you want to be sitting down with your actual game at whatever stage it's at, with a good surface to lay out what you're working on.

When working on your game, it's important to make sure you have no distractions. It's just about you and your game. Shut off all notifications. That includes email, texts, Facebook, and anything else that might take away your attention. Find a quiet space where there's nothing else for you to do except work on your game.

It might help to put up a "do not disturb" sign, and you'll definitely want to let others such as your partner and kids know that this is a dedicated time for you to work. You may want to set down a ground rule such as no interruptions except in the case of fire, or maybe an offer to play a game of Pandemic – kidding!

THE RESISTANCE

No, I'm not talking about the game. Although it definitely is a lot of fun.

I'm talking about the resistance in all of us. The self-doubt. The push-back. This is the feeling inside that will make you feel like you just can't do whatever you're trying to set your mind to. Writers refer to this as writer's block. It happens a lot in all creative endeavours.

The resistance is a term discussed in detail by Steven Pressfield in his book *The War of Art,* which is a fantastic book that all artists, writers, and anyone in business should read. There will be times that you feel like you're making no progress, or that you should give up. This is the resistance in action.

It doesn't want you to succeed. It wants to maintain the status quo. Pressfield suggests, "Most of us have two lives. The life we live, and the unlimited life within us." We sometimes have to do the things that are hard or uncomfortable for us.

Giving up on your game, or anything else you do, is taking the easy way out. You have to be consistent and keep working at it every day to see it through to completion. "The best and only thing an artist can do for another is to serve as an example and an inspiration," Pressfield states.

"But my game is no good," you say. "What right do I have to create something new?" you ask. "There are so many other game designers who are way better than me." If you're feeling any of these things, don't worry. It's normal. It's called impostor syndrome.

You may feel that everyone else is better than you, and question whether this is really what you should be doing. But remember, Eric Lang and Matt Leacock were also once unknown. Now they are famous board game designers. You can bet that they questioned themselves, especially early on in their careers.

You may not be an expert, but if you keep doing what you're doing, you'll be well on your way to becoming one! Just keep pushing ahead and know that your game is improving every day just because you keep showing up. Never give up and never give in.

In the next chapter, we'll talk about how to keep motivated, even when you don't feel like working on your game.

ACTION: Write down when and where you will work on your board game. Jot down times that you might be able to squeeze in brainstorming and testing out ideas.

If you live with others, discuss the importance of this protected time and make sure to get their support. Between you, figure out how to best allow you the time needed to work on, and create your game. Let others know you're unavailable during this time. Having this dedicated time, as well as a strong support system will put you in a great position to moving your game closer to completion every day!

CHAPTER 6
FINDING MOTIVATION TO WORK ON YOUR GAME

"Our greatest weakness lies in giving up. The most certain way to succeed is always to try just one more time."

- Thomas Edison

I won't sugarcoat it. Designing a board game can be hard. It's easy to lose your motivation and put it aside for a while. The problem is that setting a game aside for a few days can turn into a week, weeks can turn into months, and months can turn into years or you may simply never return to your board game again.

Designing a board game can and should be fun, but it is also a lot of hard work. You have to continuously playtest your game, gather feedback (much of which can and should be critical), problem solve, make changes, and repeat. There are often times where you just don't know where to take your game next. You get stuck and you don't know how to fix that nagging problem that playtesters keep identifying.

It's so much easier to just veg out with some video games or put on Netflix. There's a lot less effort involved here and humans often naturally take the path of least resistance.

But people are also driven by the need to learn and grow. That's where game design fits in. Designing a board game makes you think both creatively and logically. You're also constantly problem solving.

When you finally figure out an elegant solution to that problem you've been struggling with, it's a moment of exhilaration. When you take that game from an idea all the way to a finished product, you'll feel a tremendous sense of accomplishment.

So, let's talk about what motivation is and how to find it.

WHAT IS MOTIVATION?

First we need to start with the question of what is motivation.

According to Verywellmind.com's excellent article on motivation (https://www.verywellmind.com/what-is-motivation-2795378):

"Motivation is the process that initiates, guides, and maintains goal-oriented behaviors. It is what causes you to act, whether it is getting a glass of water to reduce thirst or reading a book to gain knowledge.

Motivation involves the biological, emotional, social, and cognitive forces that activate behavior. In everyday usage, the term 'motivation' is frequently used to describe why a person does something. It is the driving force behind human actions."

The article linked to above does a great job of explaining motivation, so I'm going to refer to some thoughts from there throughout this chapter.

SHOULD MOTIVATION BE INTERNAL OR EXTERNAL?

There are two types of motivation, intrinsic (internal) and extrinsic (external).

Extrinsic motivations are mostly driven by rewards and praise, whereas intrinsic motivations come from within, most related to personal gratification.

Think about when you're playing your favorite board game and you figure out a strategy or solve a puzzle that nobody else at the table was able to figure out. You'll be feeling clever, smart, and have a sense of personal gratification as a result.

Extrinsic motivation is often referred to as the "carrot and stick" model, where you get a carrot for carrying out good behavior or face the stick when you don't accomplish something.

When it comes to game design, you're probably doing this for your own reasons. There's usually not somebody waiting with a carrot for when your game is done, nor is there somebody holding a stick over you, forcing you to make it.

While there is a possibility that your game will go on to get signed by a publisher or maybe you'll successfully crowdfund it one day, that's probably a long way off and may never actually happen. So, it's much better to focus on intrinsic motivation - feeling good about solving a problem or taking your game the next step closer to being finished.

Notice that motivation is all about the reasons that somebody does something.

So, you need to find a way to stay self-motivated.

FINDING YOUR MOTIVATION

Getting stuck on some aspect of your game is perfectly normal. It happens to all game designers.

If you find yourself feeling stuck when you're working on your game and don't know how to continue or even if you want to, think back to why you started working on your game in the first place.

Did you want to create the game that you wanted to play but didn't exist?

Did you see a problem with another game and want to make a better version of it?

Do you just love games so much that you wanted to get more involved by making one of your own?

Did you want to challenge yourself and your creativity to see if you could take an idea and make it into something real that people would enjoy?

Maybe you couldn't find a kids game that was appealing to both you and your child and wanted to create something that you could enjoy together.

Whatever the reason you decided to make your first board game, come back to this and ask yourself if anything has changed. Do you still want to make a game, and if so, is it for the same reasons? Have those reasons changed?

What was your initial motivation and can you go back to this to feel motivated once again?

You can't rely on other people to make you feel motivated to do something, whether it is designing a board game or any other endeavor. You have to really want it yourself.

Remember that you're never doing this alone. Do you know the best way to get others to help you? In chapter 7, I'll show you.

And if you want even more help with your game, check out the resources and courses available at boardgamedesigncourse.com.

ACTION: What was your motivation for designing your board game?

Identify the reasons you began this project in the first place and see if those motivations still hold.

Keep working on your game and remember back to that feeling when you were able to fix a problem you thought couldn't be solved. That feeling of accomplishment can be felt throughout the course of designing a board game and will help to give you the motivation you need to keep going, even when times are tough.

CHAPTER 7
YOU HAVE TO GIVE BEFORE YOU GET (HELP OTHERS FIRST)

"The purpose of life is not to be happy. It is to be useful, to be honorable, to be compassionate, to have it make some difference that you have lived and lived well."

- Ralph Waldo Emerson

Helping others is not only the right thing to do, it will also benefit you in the end. That's what this chapter is all about.

PLAYTEST FOR OTHERS

You'll definitely get a lot more out of the board game community if you focus on giving back. When it comes to playtesting sessions, offer to play another designer's game first before breaking yours out.

The more helpful you are to others, the more they'll want to help you. Nobody likes that designer who only wants to play his or her own game. Besides, there are tremendous benefits to playtesting other people's games and becoming a part of a larger group.

One way you can really help other game designers is by asking the right questions. Ask about his or her game, and what they want to accomplish with it.

If they are running a playtest and don't provide that much detail, but rather just break out the game to play, ask what the goal of this playtest is. The more information you have up front, the more you can help them out. Maybe they're not exactly sure what they need to be testing, and that's where you can step in and help them figure this out.

When providing other board game designers with feedback, make sure it's helpful. You want to be honest, but not hurtful. The board game community may seem large, but it's quite small in relation to a lot of other things. Develop a reputation as a helpful playtester and fellow game designer.

You can really help other designers by giving them things to consider, and potential options. If possible, don't just point out problems you have with their game, try to come up with some creative solutions that the designer may want to try, or suggest other games that might help get them thinking in a new way.

When you're playtesting for other designers, this is a great opportunity to learn what works, and what doesn't. You'll want to take these lessons and apply them to your own playtests. This is invaluable information.

Watch a great designer playtest one of their own games. Observe how they extract helpful feedback, interact with the players, and try to use these same techniques when you're playtesting your own games.

ALWAYS BE LEARNING

There are a ton of great board game communities online as well as in cities and towns across the world. One of those communities you may consider being a part of, if you're not already, is Boardgamegeek.

This is unquestionably the largest online board game community in the world. You'll find a lot of helpful information, hundreds of thousands of fellow gamers visiting the site every day, board game contests, and anything else you can think of related to board games. Get involved here. Learn from others and contribute wherever you can. However, be warned that this site can lead to information overload.

You may also want to join some board game forums and groups. There are a lot of choices, including many Facebook game designer groups (the Board Game Design Lab is my favourite), Reddit pages, and many others. Here you will find plenty of other board game fanatics, and lots of learning opportunities.

I suggest you test the waters and explore a number of these to see which ones are of interest to you. Some of these websites and groups are friendlier and more accepting than others, and you may find that some are dominated by hard-core hobbyists and others who may shun fans of certain games or genres. Just be aware of this.

There are a lot of great blog posts related to game design as well. Some of these include blogs by Jamey Stegmaier and other creators, including myself. Search for ones that you find helpful, and join their mailing lists so that you get automatic updates. That way you never have to remember to look back for the great content they provide.

You should also keep your ear out for a number of great podcasts available. One of the best ones in my opinion is the Board Game Design Lab. It may also be worth having a listen to Ludology, Dice Tower, along with Funding the Dream (particularly if you're interested in Kickstarter). Many others out there may also be worth a look. Just search online for board game design or board game design podcasts. Check out the resources section at the back of this book for a listing of helpful books, blogs, and podcasts.

I've also got tons of free resources and blogs on topics ranging from game design to crowdfunding and everything in between that you can find on boardgamedesigncourse.com.

You may also decide to read and watch some board game reviews and play throughs. These will give you a good idea of how to explain the rules and gameplay for your own game, which can be incredibly valuable for when you're running your own playtests.

They will also show you what games are popular, what mechanics are being used, and some interesting games you might want to try yourself. Rahdo (Richard Ham), Shut Up & Sit Down, and Dice Tower are among the most popular reviewers. However, there are always new reviewers entering the space, so there's plenty of selection to find whatever you're looking for.

CONTRIBUTE

Reciprocity is a wonderful thing. By contributing and giving value to others, you can build loyalty, trust, and a strong following. You'll get more by giving first.

Be the person that others look to for answers. Once you've gained enough knowledge and feel comfortable talking about a subject, share whatever you've learned. You never know who might be listening, or who might later buy your game because of your help or advice.

If you find a great resource about board game design that you think others may be interested in but unaware of, make sure to share this. Whether it's an article, podcast, website or other helpful industry news, many designers will be very appreciative of you sharing this information.

Make sure when you share, that you're not just promoting your own game or products. That can be a big turnoff. You want to be sharing something of value. If you can relate this to something you're working on without using shameless marketing, then by all means go ahead and make this linkage.

Be willing and open to giving feedback. As I mentioned, it takes a community to create a board game. Just as you will have questions, other game designers, even experienced ones, need feedback and insights from others to make their game the best it can be.

You'll quite often see requests to review a Kickstarter page or provide feedback on a campaign within board game forums. Designers may ask all sorts of questions, put out polls, or ask for advice when dealing with a specific situation.

If you can help them, even in a small way, do whatever you can. This might involve answering a question or reviewing a rulebook. Even if it's something as simple as answering a request about whether the game box looks better in blue or red. Every little bit helps.

Share your experiences as well. What's working with your game design, and what's not; things you've discovered or learned from your playtesting sessions; discussions you've had with other designers that have led to some real insights; any learnings you've had along the way, through research or other means; any tips you have on prototyping and game design; or thanking anyone who helped you with your own game.

If you attended a convention or event, let other people know about it. What did you learn? What were your takeaways? Would you have done anything different?

I also strongly suggest you start your own blog, podcast, or video series. This is especially true if you're planning on self-publishing or using crowdfunding. In these cases, you need to develop a following and fan base. The best way to do that is to provide value to others, which will often be rewarded with loyal followers.

Have you noticed any gaping holes in game design discussions or with the information you've seen available? Do you have some really helpful tips or techniques you can share with others? Figure out how to provide value, and give back to the community. This will pay off in many ways in the future.

THEN, ASK FOR HELP

One of the mistakes I made was asking questions before first helping others. If you're new to something, and there are others whom you consider experts, or who are at least more experienced than you, then it is natural for you to approach them for advice. But you'll want to find ways you can be helpful too, even in some of the small ways I've previously mentioned.

If you have the opportunity, talk to other designers in person. They've been there, done that, and have the t-shirt. You may find some who have successfully pitched to publishers, or run Kickstarter campaigns. This is a great opportunity to ask them questions and learn from their adventures.

Most designers are very willing to talk about their experiences, and help steer you in the right direction. They can let you know about any pitfalls you may not have considered, and let you know about other options you didn't know existed.

Other board game designers are there to help you. The great thing about the board game community is that it's really not all that competitive, at least at the board game designer level (this may be a different story at the publishing level however...).

Designers just really want to promote the hobby. There's plenty of space for your game, their game, and everyone else's game. The goal is to get more people interested in playing board games. Period.

Most designers will readily give you advice that can be very helpful, along with recommendations for publishers who are good to work with, high quality manufacturers, and other inside information. You can ask them just about anything related to their experiences running a Kickstarter campaign or pitching to publishers. Board game designers love talking about what they do. Just be ready to do a lot of listening!

If you post a question in one of the board game forums, you're almost guaranteed to get a response. Most of these forums are very active, and there's always somebody ready to give you their opinion or advice. Keep in mind however, that not all advice is good, and you have to use your own judgment. However, if you're getting a lot of consistent responses, they should be taken into consideration.

As mentioned, other designers sometimes use polls in these forums to gauge interest and get feedback. This is definitely something you can take advantage of as well. If you have five potential names for your game, you can always post them and ask people to vote on their favourite. You can do the same with art, design, or many other aspects of game creation. This will not only give you valuable information, but will also help you engage with the community, and potentially gain more interest in your game.

When you're reaching out on these forums, you'll often be talking to those in the know. You may even get a response from a game designer whose game you've played. Many are quite active in the community, and willing to help aspiring designers with questions they have.

There are also many people who are just as new to game design as you. Over time, you'll get to know the experienced and really helpful game designers in the community.

So now you're getting involved, generating ideas, and really thinking hard about what your game will be all about. So, should you focus on one idea or have multiple on the go that you can bounce between? That's the topic of our next chapter.

ACTION: Look online for board game design blogs, podcasts, and websites, including those I've mentioned (and check the Resources section at the back of this book as well). Read or listen to the content available here, and join those lists you think will be helpful to you.

Also look into the various forums mentioned as well as others you may find. If you are interested, join these and see what people are posting there. Become an active member, make comments, and help others where you can.

CHAPTER 8
WORKING ON ONE GAME VS. MANY

"I think it's wrong that only one company makes the game Monopoly."

— Steven Wright, comedian

After you start working on your first game, you may be tempted to switch your focus to another game idea that comes to mind. While this new game concept may be amazing, I strongly recommend that you continue to focus on your game at hand, at least until your first game is done. Once you have your first game finished, you may choose to have more than one project on the go.

I have to admit that this is one of the areas that I struggle with the most when it comes to board game design. If you're like me, you'll start seeing board game ideas everywhere, and will be excited by every new thought that comes into your head. I have to make a conscious effort to not jump continuously from one new idea to the next, and I'm about to explain why.

WHY FOCUS ON ONE?

One of the problems with working on more than one thing at a time is that you may never finish your first project. In fact, you may never finish any project. I strongly suggest you get one board game finished and under your belt before you start doing any serious work on your next game.

At the very least, it will give you a great feeling of accomplishment. Think about it. You'll put in all this time and effort, and as a result, you'll have a finished, playable game to show for it. Even if it's not the best game ever, it's still done. Very few people in the world can say they've actually created a board game, but you'll be able to.

It's also a lot easier to concentrate on one game as opposed to many. There's a whole lot less confusion about where you left off and what you need to do next. If you start splitting your attention between multiple projects, there's a strong chance you'll end up with the shelf full of partially completed games. You will have put in a lot of hard work, but won't have anything to show for it.

This may even discourage you to the point that you give up on game design altogether. It's easy to start a game, but much more difficult to finish one.

By following the steps outlined in this book to turn your idea into a final, playable game, you'll also be training your brain to follow a proven method. This will make future games that much easier to work through.

IT'S REALLY EASY TO GET DISTRACTED

There's a condition that a lot of people have nowadays. It's called "shiny object syndrome." Game designers are no different. You see something new and awesome, and you get distracted from the task at hand. Believe me, I've been there. There's always a new technology, gadget, board game, or idea that suddenly appears and it looks so amazing!

The next big thing or new idea is always so appealing. This is just human nature. New is fresh. Exciting. It's what everyone wants.

There's nothing wrong with appreciating something fresh or innovative, but we can't let this distract us from our main priority. Just remember, that idea will still be there when you're done your game. You can always come back to it later.

You'll also find that it's much easier to tinker around with a new idea than to fix an existing problem. Fixing problems is hard. Playing around with something new seems so much easier and more fun.

But we can't just walk away from our problems, because they'll still be there. And with that new idea, you'll eventually run into a completely different set of obstacles.

If you continue this cycle, you'll be left with a whole whack of problems, and it may seem too daunting to come back and fix any one of them. Don't worry, the solution to your problem **will** come to you. You're smart. After all, you're a game designer!

Remember that distractions are just another form of procrastination and resistance. Your brain wants a break. It wants to do something easy. It doesn't want to continue working away at something hard. You've got to fight back against the resistance!

One book that I would suggest reading is *Getting Things Done* by David Allen. In the book, Allen goes over methods to get ideas out of your head so that rather than continuing to think about them, you can prioritize and get things done (as the title suggests!). This has helped me to focus on many aspects of my life, not only game design. As a result, I am able to get a lot more done and stay focused on what matters.

Getting distracted and taking your focus away from the game you're working on to look at something else is just procrastination. Be consistent and keep working away at it. You'll get there.

YOU CAN WORK ON MULTIPLE GAMES LATER

You plan to design many more games over time, not just one game, right? If you've read this far, I have to believe that you're a board game designer and not just some guy or gal with one, and only one, idea.

As I mentioned earlier, there will be a time that it may be beneficial to work on more than one game at a time. However, this depends on a number of factors, but primarily by what type of game designer you are.

Some people focus strictly on one game at a time, taking it from idea to completion, before starting on their next project. But many designers have multiple games in progress, all at various stages. What approach you take is up to you, although I will again strongly advise that you take your first game from start to finish, focusing on this game alone, before working on any other games.

Having said this, if you have an idea for a new game, by all means write it down! Otherwise, that idea will likely be lost. Save this idea for the future. It will still be there later when you're done your first game, just waiting for you. You'll say "Oh yeah! I forgot all about that. I want to work on that one next!"

You may have a whole list of ideas by the time your first game is done, which is a great position to be in. You'll be able to evaluate all of these ideas, and decide which one is the most interesting to you, or has the most potential as a board game. Your first game is just a start. You have the potential to create **many** great games in your game design career.

As I mentioned, one of my biggest struggles is dealing with all the ideas I come up with, and having to train myself to focus on one of these at a time. However, this is not a bad problem to have. I always have something else to work on if I ever need to take a break from my current game, and it also gives me lots of different options I can discuss with various publishers. I don't just have one game in the works to offer.

After focusing completely on my first game, and only jotting down ideas for other games at the time, I now have a long list of games that I'm working on simultaneously. Personally, I love this variety. However, I'm really glad that I took my first game to a finished stage before doing any real work on any of the others.

Once you're at this stage, having the ability to jump between games can be a lot of fun. If you're stuck, you can take your mind off the problem and work on another game, which could result in a solution to your original problem, or at least other possibilities.

Again, I only suggest doing this once you've completed your first game. Being able to say you've actually created a board game is an amazing thing. It will just lead you to want to make more. At least I sure hope so!

The other dilemma that some designers find themselves in is quite the opposite; they are stuck at some point in their game design and can't move forward. Chapter 9 is all about how to get unstuck.

ACTION: Commit to finishing your first game before working on any others. Keep a notebook, Excel sheet, or whatever means will help you to track new ideas. You'll want to come back to this once you're done your first game, so that you will have plenty of ideas for your next endeavour.

CHAPTER 9
GETTING UNSTUCK

"Genius is one percent inspiration, ninety nine percent perspiration."

– Thomas Edison

There will be times when you will be stuck while working on your game. This is natural. As with any creative endeavour, there will be times when things aren't quite working right, or you're not sure of the next step. I'll outline a number of things you can do to get yourself unstuck when you find yourself in these situations, and help keep your game moving forward.

PLAY GAMES (YES, AGAIN...)

I know I've mentioned that it's good to play a lot of games to give you a broader perspective as well as some ideas for your own games, but you may also find it helpful to play games when you're stuck. Play not only good games that you like, but also some bad ones.

The good ones will help you to discover what works, along with some possible ideas and mechanics you can use to help you enhance the player experience and fix any issues you're working on. It's also just as important to play some bad games as well. This will give you ideas of what not to do in a game, which can save you a lot of time and be equally helpful.

Make sure to include both published games and games in the playtesting stage. Published games should be complete and play well, although you'll run into the occasional game that feels broken in some way. You'll want to ask the question "why is this game working and what did they do right in the design?" This will help you apply some of the same concepts in your game.

By playtesting lots of prototypes, you'll see games at all stages. Some might be further along than yours, and others may be in an earlier phase. Some may be close to completion, which will allow you to imagine where your game will be in the near future.

Playtesting games for others will allow you to see other innovative approaches, mechanics, and themes that other designers have applied to their own games. In the design process, you'll always be learning, and this will be another great opportunity to generate ideas.

But don't just play the newest, hottest game out there. You want to play a combination of new and old games.

Understand how games have changed over time. What are players' expectations nowadays? What is still common between a lot of these games? It's helpful to see the good and the bad (and sometimes even the ugly!) to know when to apply certain techniques in your own game.

TAKE A BREAK

Go for a walk, get some exercise, and enjoy some fresh air. It can be really helpful to take yourself out of one environment and put yourself in a new one.

You may get a new perspective, and find this invigorating. Ideas may come to you, or you may just find yourself in a different, more positive state of mind. The fresh air is also great for your health and well-being.

While your game design will be done predominantly indoors, you want to make sure you're still taking care of yourself and interacting with the rest the world. Don't become a hermit!

You can also try doing something mundane, like washing dishes, folding laundry, or some other household task that doesn't require much thought. You'll be surprised what a difference this can make. Ideas might come to you while you're doing these chores, or when you return fresh to your game.

Do you have a place of inspiration? Go there. Relax and do what you normally would do in this inspirational place. Hopefully the ideas will come to you naturally. Don't force it!

TALK IT OUT WITH SOMEONE

Have you ever noticed how talking out a problem or issue with someone usually makes you feel better? This seems to lessen the burden and takes a great weight off your shoulders.

Sometimes an idea will come to you in the middle of explaining the situation. Just getting this off your chest and verbalizing it can often lead you to thinking of a brand new approach you can take.

When you share this problem with someone else, they may have ideas or advice for you as well. They might suggest something that they've seen done in another game that deals with a similar issue that you've never played before. Understanding what other designers have done when confronting challenges can make it easier for you to address a specific issue.

This friend or acquaintance may even take a completely different approach and apply your problem to something they are more familiar with, which is completely unrelated. This may lead to a unique way of thinking about it.

If the other person you're talking to is a board game designer, this can be even more helpful. They have often dealt with similar issues. They will also likely be more than willing to share what they've tried, and what's worked for them. You are probably not the only person to run into this type of dilemma. Sometimes it's great when you don't have to reinvent the wheel!

FIGHTING THE RESISTANCE

I know I'm repeating myself, but you really do have to be consistent. Continue to put in the time, working on your game regularly.

Even if you don't feel like you're making great progress, remember that you're honing your skills and becoming a better game designer all the time. This will allow you to come to solutions more readily. It's all about staying in the game… pun intended.

Don't let the resistance win. Keep trying new things. Test any idea, even a crazy one. Collect your playtesting notes and see if there's anything you missed, or anything that was suggested that would be worth trying.

Focus on the most fun part of your game. What aspect of the game is really conveying that player experience that you're aiming for? What part do players really enjoy? This is the area that you want to focus on.

Try turning the problem on its head. If you've got a cooperative game, think about how it might work as a competitive game. How would it look if players were in a different or opposite role than they are currently in? Or you could work on another aspect of the game, and come back to this later. Just keep moving your game forward!

FIND OUT WHAT WORKS FOR YOU, AND MAKE NOTE OF THIS

Being stuck and not knowing what you should do next is not a place you want to stay for very long. Write down whatever has helped you get out of this stage. Return to this place the next time you're stuck. It may not always work but it's certainly worth a try.

Maybe for you it's walking. It could be driving. Rob Daviau, the designer of many legacy games, finds it helpful to take a drive, but, when he does, he can only listen to classical music. If he listens to rock, he'll want to sing along, and this will obviously not be the most helpful way to find a solution to the problem he's working on!

What about relaxing and daydreaming? You can't work all the time. Besides, creativity is hard to harness if you're focused on working all the time.

Allow yourself the time to step away from whatever you're doing and take some time to daydream. Where do you see yourself in the future? What if this game becomes really successful? Picture what that would mean for you.

The answer to your challenge is not likely to come to you when you're sitting at a computer banging your head against the keyboard. Sometimes you just have to get up and take a break. Discover where you find your solutions, and when the best ideas come to you. Yes, take a break, but always remember to come back to your game!

So, what's going to make your game stand out against all the others? How do professional board game designers do it? I'll let you in on this in the next section.

ACTION: Determine the ways that help you get unstuck. If you're having a challenge with your game, talk it out with someone, whether it be a spouse, friend, family member, or another game designer. Don't let this temporary setback hold you down!

SECTION 3

KEY ELEMENTS AND CONSIDERATIONS

CHAPTER 10
YOUR VISION FOR YOUR GAME

"Use those talents you have. You will make it. You will give joy to the world. Take this tip from nature: The woods would be a very silent place if no birds sang except those who sang best."

- Bernard Meltzer, entertainer

Now we get to the fun stuff – we're going to really get into the nuts and bolts of designing your own board game. In this chapter, and the following chapters in this section, you'll start to get a good feel for what your game will look like, and what elements it will include. This is a really good starting point for getting your game to the table faster.

UNDERSTAND YOUR VISION

It's important to know from a fairly early stage in your board game design what the vision is for your game. Once you have this figured out, you'll want to write it down, so you can always refer back to it. When you have to start making hard decisions about what to cut or change in your game, you will use this as your compass. In this way, your game will retain its "soul."

You want to figure out what the key elements are for your game. What's your game about? Most importantly, what are the **feelings** and **experiences** you want players to have when they play your game. I'll go into this crucial aspect of your game in more depth shortly. For now, think about what parts of your game you will not waver on. While other elements may be added and removed as you're going through the process, you'll want to hold firm on the aspects you won't compromise on.

Always remember that it's **your** game. Ultimately, you make the final decisions about what changes and what remains in your game.

A word of caution: If this is the first board game you've ever created, I suggest keeping it relatively uncomplicated. This will keep the scope of your game reasonable, and allow you to get your first game done with minimal headaches. If you decide to create a heavy Euro game with lots of "moving parts" as your first game, you may be in for a long haul and may not follow through.

BE PREPARED TO MAKE A LOT OF CHANGES

Through the course of creating and improving your game, you'll be doing a lot of playtesting and asking for feedback. As your game gets closer to completion and you gain more experience, you'll be able to tell more easily what feedback will make your game different versus making your game better. While making your game different may be interesting, what we are ultimately aiming to do is make your game better with every iteration.

You're going to get lots of suggestions. Always be open to the suggestions you receive, and make sure to thank friends, playtesters, and other designers who take the time to give you their honest impressions and advice. Just remember that you don't have to use every suggestion that you're given.

What you want to do at first is focus on the problems rather than the solutions. Ultimately, the solution is for you to discover. Other designers may come up with some good recommendations as well, which you may want to consider more strongly than suggestions from playtesters, simply because they have more game design experience.

NOTHING LIKE WHAT YOU IMAGINED

I've come across lots of examples of games that have changed quite a bit from the original concept to where they are now. This includes a number of my own games, along with games from other designers that I've had the pleasure to playtest.

I once playtested a game by a couple of local designers that I think you'll agree has changed significantly. The original theme was based on rap battles, but evolved over time to become a game centred on an occult theme, where players take on the roles of historical mediums and clair-voyants, trying to gain more followers than their opponents. Talk about a drastic shift!

Have you ever played the game *Lanterns* by Chris Chung? This was Chris's first published game and has become a huge success. It is themed around the Chinese Lantern Festival, but when it was first handed over to the publisher, it was more of an abstract game. The publisher added this compelling theme to the game, which made it even more interesting. The core of the game remained the same; however, the theme made this even more appealing to players.

Here's an example from a game I'm co-designing called *Isle of Rock 'n Roll*, in which players form bands and compete for world domination. This game has changed dramatically in the way it's played over many years and way too many playtests. Originally, players drew cards to form their bands, but this felt too luck-based, and quickly evolved to a pick-and-pass drafting mechanic, similar to *Sushi Go* or *7 Wonders*. I then tried a tableau structure with players drafting band members. I added gigs, and tried a bunch of other ideas that came from playtesting, some of which worked, and some of which didn't.

Years later, we're still tinkering with this, trying to find the right balance of simplicity and challenge. We've definitely made some huge strides with this and cut out some aspects that would have added a lot of production cost without the equivalent amount of fun. It's still a work in progress and may or may not ever be published and you have to be ok with this. Not every game gets published or should be published.

Your game could end up looking quite different from the original idea you had in your head. Perhaps the theme will change over time. Maybe you'll add or switch out a mechanic or the gameplay will be changed entirely.

Anything can happen over the course of playtesting and iterating. It is ultimately up to you what direction the game takes next, but don't be surprised if the end result looks quite different from your first idea.

BUT REMEMBER TO STICK TO YOUR OVERALL VISION

While it's true that your game will change quite a bit over time, there are some elements you **won't** want to change. While it's interesting to think about something that would take it in a very different direction, this would also make it a totally different game. It might be better to jot this idea down for now and possibly apply it to a new game concept in the future. For now, you want to stick to the vision for your game.

If your game isn't going quite the way you want, try to identify and change what isn't working. Just remember to know and understand what you will and won't compromise on. You don't **have** to change something just because somebody suggested it, even if it sounds like a cool idea. Remember your vision, and stick to your guns!

The next chapter is all about what will set your game apart from every other game. I'll give you a hint: it's not about how "fun" your game is.

ACTION: What is your overall vision for your game? What won't you compromise on? The next chapter and the following chapters will help you to refine this. For now, just list the key elements and aspects of your game that are most important to you.

CHAPTER 11
PLAYER EXPERIENCE AND FEELING

"How the players feel during your game is far more important than if the game is about Cthulu or if worker placement is your main mechanic. First, figure out what you want players to experience, and then build out your theme and mechanics to achieve that experience."

– Gabe Barrett, Founder of The Board Game Design Lab

We're about to get into a crucial element of game design. This one thing will help guide every choice you make in designing your game. Let's get right to it!

UNDERSTANDING THE PLAYER EXPERIENCE IS KEY

What experience do you want players to have when they're playing your game? What feelings are you aiming for as they explore the dungeon you created, or come up with zany answers in your party game? These are the types of questions you need to ask in order to ensure your game is hitting the mark.

"Well, I want players to have fun," you might say. Don't get me wrong. Fun is great, but it's also very subjective. Ultimately, you want players to have a fun experience, but this can come in many different ways. The fun aspect of playing *Cards Against Humanity* is very different from what is fun about *Catan*. As you develop your game, you need to determine what exactly is "fun" about it.

TYPES OF PLAYER EXPERIENCES AND FEELINGS

Many different player experiences and feelings can come through in games. I have included some below. This is by no means a complete list, rather some examples you may want to consider:

- Calm and peaceful

- Frantic

- Smart

- Challenged

- Creative

- Embarrassed

- Accomplished

- Frightened

- Cooperative and helpful

ONE WAY TO GET IDEAS

If you're really having difficulty coming up with an idea of what you want your players to experience in your game, one method would be to look at a random idea generator such as the one at Lets Make a Game (https://letsmakeagame.net/game-idea-generator/) or others available online (see resources section at the back of this book).

This is a great site, as it will randomly generate genre, rule, setting, and theme for a potential game. We'll get more into these and other categories in a moment. This may give you a great idea for a feeling and game related to this, or lead you to think of something else based on the suggestions it proposes.

Here are a few examples that I randomly generated:

#1

Genre: Farming

Rule: Start Small

Setting: High Fantasy

Theme: Race to the Finish

#2

Genre: Puzzle

Rule: Death is Good

Setting: Simulated Reality

Theme: Search for Identity

#3

Genre: Tower Defense

Rule: Keep it Alive

Setting: Zombie

Theme: Pursuit

Some pretty interesting things could come from the above combinations or ones you generate on your own!

MORE IMPORTANT THAN THEME AND MECHANICS

If you're able to come up with a vision for your game, including what experience you want players to feel, this will really help determine what theme and mechanics you'll want to use. You may find the theme and mechanics naturally follow in order to help attain the experience you're aiming for. This isn't to say that you can't start with theme or mechanics, but it's often easier and more helpful to start with an overall idea for your player experience first.

Here are some examples of different player experiences/feelings (this is just a sample – there are so many that you could use!), including some games that make use of these:

- **Humour and Laughter** – Examples: *Cards Against Humanity, Snake Oil, Cranium.* These games are very light in terms of complexity, are easy to learn, and produce many funny, memorable moments. For example, the aim of *Cards Against Humanity* is for people to feel shocked, and have some laughs over the inappropriate responses that players choose. This is attained through an adult theme, and the simple pick, pass, and judge mechanics.

- **Calming** – Examples: *Patchwork, Tsuro.* These games are generally played at a slow pace, provide a relaxing experience, and use easy to understand mechanics involving selecting from a small number of choices and playing a tile or piece.

- **Frantic** – Examples: *Dutch Blitz, Escape: Curse of the Temple, Fuse.* These games are fast-paced, with little time to think, and often use a timer, along with dice or cards. Players have to make quick decisions, and all players are taking actions simultaneously. In *Fuse* for example, the theme revolves around disabling bombs, which immediately makes you think of something you have to do very quickly to avoid catastrophe. It also accomplishes this goal through the mechanics of simultaneous dice rolling and a timer to great effect.

- **Cooperation and Teamwork** – Examples: *Pandemic, Flashpoint: Fire Rescue, Forbidden Island.* These are generally team-based, rescue-themed or similar, where everyone must work together under some sense of pressure. There are many things that all players have to do, but each can only do so much on their turn. The themes used in these games, such as rescuing people from a burning building, or even saving the entire world, ensure co-operation and teamwork. The mechanics used in these games increase the pressure over time, and the only way to win is by working together.

- **Smart** – Examples: *Splendor, 7 Wonders, Santorini*. Many of these games are very strategic, and there's a real sense of accomplishment when you see your strategy succeed. These are often engine–building games that ramp up and rely on players making tough decisions. They use related themes such as building or creating something, or perhaps a more abstract theme, using mechanics to allow players to continue to create that structure or thing, building up to a climax where one player claims victory.

- **Sneaky** – Examples: *Cheaty Mages, Munchkin, Fluxx*. These are often "take that" types of games that typically involve sabotaging other players' plans in some manner, or changing the rules in your favour. Often card-based games, they typically use themes involving sneaky characters or rules, such as thieves or other backstabbing characters. The action mechanics of the game allow players to do things to help themselves or hinder others.

ALL DECISIONS WILL REVOLVE AROUND THIS

The great thing about having a clear vision for your game and understanding the experience you want players to have is that it makes it much easier to create your game and make decisions about what direction you want to take.

Say you get feedback or suggestions from a playtesting session. You can ask yourself the simple question: "Does this align with my vision and the experience I want players to have?" If so, then it may be worth trying that idea. If not, the suggestion, while interesting, may not be that helpful to you. You'll only focus on making changes that will help enhance the player experience, not stray from your vision.

So when you're doing your playtesting, you should be asking yourself whether the suggestions enhance the experience or not.

Make sure to hold to your vision. The player experience and feeling are the most important aspects of your game. You may get some great unexpected suggestions, but if they take your game away from the direction you are intending, it may turn this into a very different game.

That's not to say that this information isn't helpful. You may take this idea and create a completely new game based on it. You may even decide that this is a better direction for your game, however I caution you to try to work with your original vision first. But if you find that your game's just not working, it may be worth looking again at this other idea. Just don't jump ship too early and abandon what could have been a great game.

PLAYER EXPERIENCE AND FEELING DETERMINE THE STORY AND ROLES FOR THE PLAYERS

What's the story in your game? What roles will players portray in that story? The player experience you have in mind can really help you determine exactly what this story is.

Consider which perspective you're taking with this game. This can vary greatly from one game to the next. For example, if you're making a game that is sports-related, you may consider players taking on the role of player, coach, or general manager.

If you are creating a superhero type of game, your players could be either the good guys or the bad guys, or perhaps some players will be assigned to each role. It's interesting to look at various perspectives and see how you can create a game in a way that's different than all the others out there.

This will also help determine the direction of your game. It's going to look very different if players are taking on the role of a villain or bad guy as opposed to a good guy or hero. As you're playtesting your game, you can start by asking the question: "Is this something someone in this role would want to do or have as an option?" By understanding the exact role that players are taking on, this will make a lot more sense. If they're playing a good guy, then destroying City Hall wouldn't even be on their radar, whereas if they are a bad guy, this might be one of the first things they'll want to do.

Most games tend to be competitive; however, cooperative games are now being produced much more often. Which type of game is yours? Are players working against each other, or together to reach a common goal?

It could even be a semi-cooperative game, where players have to rely on each other at times, but not throughout the whole game. Note that these dynamics may change through the course of playtesting, which is fine as long as your overall vision for the game remains the same.

My friend and fellow game designer, Andy Kim (designer of *The Spill*), showed me a prototype of a game he's working on, called *Valet*. In this game, players are trying to return cars to customers quickly, in order to keep them happy and maintain a good reputation. Originally, this was a competitive game, but he found that players were taking a long time between turns, it just wasn't as fun as it should've been, and wasn't providing the same player experience he had envisioned.

After working out what some of the problems might be through numerous playtests, it suddenly dawned on him that this could work really well as a cooperative game. I had the pleasure of playtesting this new version and it definitely did work nicely as a cooperative game.

The overall vision for his game remained the same, however the way it was played changed, which actually made for a better experience. In fact, he was able to attain more of the experience that he was hoping for. This goes to show that a game can go through a major change, be made even better, and still invoke (or even improve) the player experience.

Now it's time to build a game around this player experience you have created.

ACTION: Determine what main feeling you want your players to experience in your game. Write this down. Let this be the guiding light that you follow throughout the formation of the amazing game you are about to create.

CHAPTER 12
THEME VS. MECHANICS

"Form follows function."

- Louis Henri Sullivan, architect

Theme and mechanics are other important aspects of any game. But should you focus on one more than the other? We'll discuss that next.

WHICH DO I START WITH?

There's a lot of debate in the board game design community about whether to start with theme or mechanics. I think the clear answer is there's no clear answer. Every designer and every game is different. There's no "right" way to do this. But if you start with the player experience and feel, this will help you to determine a great theme along with mechanics you can use to accomplish this goal.

WHAT ARE MECHANICS?

So what exactly are mechanics? No, I'm not talking about the guy charging you a hundred bucks to fill up your brake fluid. Mechanics are really short for mechanisms; the mechanisms by which players can do the things they need to do in order to accomplish the goals of the game.

There are plenty of different existing mechanics to choose from as well as new mechanics that are being created all the time. Many games incorporate multiple mechanics in order to achieve their desired player experience.

While mechanics are important to the game, just remember that players can only handle so much complexity before they start to tune out or get confused. You may be tempted to come up with something really unique. Remember, it's great to have an original idea, but if it is so different from anything anyone's ever seen before, it may be difficult to understand and may not be applied correctly by players.

You also don't want to introduce too many new mechanics at once. It's generally a good idea to incorporate only one new thing at a time. Otherwise you may run into player overwhelm.

Gateway games, which are games that are frequently used to introduce non-gamers to the hobby, such as *Ticket to Ride* and *Catan*, generally add one new mechanic beyond what people might be familiar with. This provides a gateway for players into potentially more complex or heavy games.

There are a lot of different mechanics you can use in a game. Rather than list them all here (which would probably double the length of this book!) I've shared with you a really helpful list in the Resources Section of this book, which includes many common mechanics used in games. I also recommend Building Blocks of Game Design, by Geoff Engelstein and Isaac Shalev, which goes very in-depth on board game mechanics.

WHAT IS THEME IN A GAME?

You'll often hear a gamer say that a particular game is very thematic. Theme can be very important in a game. It can make players feel like they are in a far-off fantasy world, or in the trenches during World War II. When this is done well, it can help to create an amazing experience for players.

The theme allows the designer to create a great story for the players. When you're creating your game, try to think of some interesting themes that can evolve from the player experience you're aiming for.

Some themes may appear to have been done to death (zombies, Cthulhu, dungeon crawls, ninjas, pirates, etc.), yet still sell well. On the other hand, there are lots of themes that have not been explored nearly as well in games. One approach you could use is to take one specific aspect of a theme, and make it different and perhaps even more interesting than the other games out there in that genre.

For instance, the game *Unbroken*, by Artem Safarov (which is still in production at the time of this writing), adopts an interesting twist on dungeon crawls. It is actually a solo adventure, and takes place just after the creatures inhabiting the dungeon have decimated the rest of your party.

You'll want to make your game something that's of interest to other players, not only fun for yourself. If you're an accountant, you may enjoy completing tax returns; however, this may not be a theme that appeals to everyone.

That being said, the game *Sagrada*, by Adrian Ademescu and Daryl Andrews, revolves around the theme of stained glass windows. Now this may not sound that exciting at first, but the artwork is beautiful, and works itself really well into the theme. While playing *Sagrada* you may not actually feel like you're creating a stained glass window, but the theme still fits nicely.

Try to avoid creating a theme that is "pasted on." By that, I mean a theme that doesn't really seem to relate to the game. If you've ever played a game where the theme really doesn't seem to matter, or even worse, detracts from the game, then you'll know what I'm talking about.

That being said, there's nothing wrong in creating an abstract game. It's often better to keep a game abstract than try to force a theme onto it that just doesn't work. There are plenty of great abstract games that have been around for a long time that don't need to rely on a theme (ever heard of *Checkers*, *Backgammon*, or *Chess*?).

If you can work a compelling theme into your game that makes sense, go for it. Just don't make it feel forced!

MECHANICS YOU MAY WANT TO AVOID

While there are many mechanics you can choose from, some of them are not the most popular mechanics (see what I did there?). Here are some mechanics (and outcomes of mechanics) that I strongly urge you to consider avoiding, or at least seriously reconsidering, in favour of mechanics that are more effective:

- **Roll and Move (or spin and move, or anything similar).** This mechanic was used a lot in older family-friendly games like *Monopoly*, *Candy Land*, and *Snakes & Ladders*. The big problem with this mechanic is that there is no choice involved. You roll. You land somewhere. Something happens. That's it. There's nothing you can do to avoid it. This makes a game completely based on luck, with little to no strategy or choice. This may be great for games intended for very young children in order to even the playing field with adults, but otherwise, avoid this at all costs. Roll and move is dead.

- **Player Elimination.** While this isn't necessarily terrible in a game that can be played in 10 minutes, consider this: have you ever been the first player out early on in a game like *Risk* or *Monopoly*? How fun is it to sit around for a couple hours while everyone else continues to play? Seriously, do you want people to **not** play your game? Because that's what you're doing. Keep everyone in the game as long as you can.

- **Miss a Turn.** Another example of getting people to **not** play your game. It can already be a drag waiting for your turn to come around, so why make someone wait even longer before they can do anything? This is a sure way to ruin someone's interest and engagement in your game.

- **Overly Harsh Consequences.** This is more of a general thing to consider, but don't make penalties in a game so harsh that people don't ever want to play again. If you send a player all the way back to the start when they were two squares away from winning, how frustrated do you think they will feel? Will they ever want to play again? Anything similar to this, like losing a key item, or having to redo what they've just spent an hour putting together, will just lead to frustration. Missing a turn sucks, so why punish players even more?

- **Any Mechanics That Lead to Long Gaps Between Turns.** Another general statement, but one of great importance. If players have a long time to wait with nothing to do between turns, they will quickly lose interest. Are your players engaged or looking for something else to do? If there's a way to keep players immersed throughout the game, especially where players have to be keeping an eye on what other players are doing, or planning their next turn, this will speed up the gameplay and definitely enhance the experience.

- **Any Mechanic, Layout or Structure that Induces Analysis Paralysis (AP).** This is a very real thing. If someone has a choice between two or three options, they may deliberate for a moment, but they will usually be able to make a decision relatively quickly. Give that same player 20 different options, and you could be in for not only long gaps between turns, but also a lot of pressure on the player, with others encouraging them to "hurry up already!" Keep the choices simple, but interesting.

It's also helpful to keep in mind that some themes and genres of games are notoriously difficult to market or get a publisher's interest. Sports games, trivia games, word games, adult-themed games, and trading card games (TCGs) are known to be difficult sales. That doesn't mean that you can't make or even get a game like this published but just know that your game will really have to stand out (more than normal) and that it may be an uphill battle.

You'll also want to ensure that all players feel that they have a chance to win. If anyone is so far behind that they know that nothing they do will change this, they will become completely disengaged. If you find this is happening in your game, you may want to introduce a "rubber band-type" catch up mechanism. In the video game world, *Super Mario Kart* does this well in that the last place player can usually get a really nice item that will let them get back in the race.

You can also use a "head wind" mechanic, which prevents the leader from getting too far ahead. Resources may get more expensive the further you are ahead or there may be some sort of taxation system that makes you pay more if you have more to begin with.

In a board game, this could be achieved through a bigger tax on higher income earners, or allowing the last place player to go first the next round if there is a distinct advantage to this. If possible, try not to make it too obvious or painful for players in the lead though.

INTERESTING DECISIONS

This is a topic that's also discussed a lot by board game designers. As mentioned previously, you don't want to have all choices predetermined for players. You want them to be able to make interesting decisions on their turn.

What do I mean by interesting decisions?

Well, first of all, you want all, or at least most of the choices, to be **viable.** If you provide a choice between three objects they can take, and one is clearly much better than the other two, then the choice is obvious. But if each of those three items has a special power that could be helpful in different ways, and the player must make a choice between them, this gives players much more to think about and a more interesting decision. Players may not have all the information they need, but they should be able to make an informed decision based on all the viable options.

The decision that a player makes should also have **impact.** If it's a decision that doesn't really have much impact in the end, what does it matter what choice they make? If the player chooses wisely, they will feel smart and strategic. If they make a choice that doesn't turn out well, they may curse themselves for the option they selected, and this may lead them to make a different choice or explore other alternatives the next time they play.

The choice should also be **meaningful.** In business there's a term called "opportunity cost." This refers to the cost of choosing one thing over another. It may be financial, or otherwise. In a game, there should be consequences to the choice being made. For instance, if you select one card, perhaps the other cards that you didn't select are no longer available, or perhaps your opponents receive them.

A good example incorporating all of these aspects comes from *7 Wonders*, in which you are dealt a handful of cards, and you can only select one before passing the rest of them to the player beside you. Whatever you do not pick, your neighbour can then take. This makes every choice important and meaningful. You're playing both offensively and defensively, which makes for a really interesting game.

The mechanics and theme you choose for your game will help lead you towards some interesting decisions that players will need to make. Ensure that players can take fate into their own hands, rather than having everything just determined by pure luck.

Speaking of luck, we'll get into luck, probability, and randomness next, along with determining how players will win, and a few other important aspects of your game that you'll want to discover.

ACTION: Now that you have a vision for your game and understand the experience and feelings you want your player to have, come up with a theme for your game, along with the mechanics you want to try in order to provide players with this experience. Remember that it's always possible to change your theme and mechanics later. For now, just get an idea of the first things you'd like to try. Soon you will begin playtesting, at which point you'll find out whether or not these themes and mechanics actually work in practice.

CHAPTER 13
THINGS TO KEEP IN MIND

*"I think that randomness in a game is very strong medicine, and
must be very carefully controlled."*

- Warren Robinett, game designer

There are a number of other things you'll want to keep in mind as you
create your board game. I'll go into these more in depth in this chapter.

HOW WILL PLAYERS WIN?

As you're working on your game, you'll want to consider what the **victory condition** is. By that, I mean how players will win the game.

You can use many possible options here, including, but not limited to,
the following (with examples in brackets):

- Most points or dollars (*7 Wonders*, *Scrabble*)

- Least points (*Hearts*)

- Winner of the most rounds, such as best two out of three games (*Jaipur*)

- First to run out of cards (*Crazy Eights*)

- First to the finish (*Snakes & Ladders*)

- First to complete the objective or a set number of objectives (*Machi Koro*)

- Last one standing (*Checkers, Monopoly*)

- First to get a set number of pieces in a row (*Tic-Tac-Toe, Connect Four*)

- Complete a task before the time runs out (*Perfection, Fuse*)

- Survive at the end with health or hit points remaining (*Dungeons & Dragons*)

- Player with the most pieces remaining (*Othello*)

- Be the last player with moves still remaining (*Chess*)

- Capture the flag/player (*Stratego*)

- A combination of these or other possible victory conditions

THE ROLE (AND ROLL) OF RANDOMNESS AND CHANCE IN YOUR GAME

Every game is different, and the role of chance may range between complete luck and pure strategy. Most games have at least some elements of both in them.

Chance, or luck, may come in the form of whether the card that will be taken from the top of the deck will help you, or whether you roll a six to defeat that nasty monster that will otherwise annihilate you in some not-so-pleasant ways!

It's helpful for you as a game designer to understand the basics of probability and how this applies to your game. Otherwise, you may end up creating decisions that nobody will choose, as the probability of something good coming from it will be so low, it's not worth it. You want to be able to balance the risk to reward ratio.

Let's take the beloved act of rolling a die. Assuming we're using a standard six-sided die (or d6), there is an equal chance that you will roll a 1, 2, 3, 4, 5, or 6. Each has a 1 in 6 or 16.7% (rounded) probability. If you want a player to have an equal chance of something good or something bad happening, you could assign 1-3 for good, and 4-6 for bad.

However, when you add a second die, something interesting happens. The distribution completely changes. Some values are now much more likely to happen than others. Let's take a look at the chart on the next page.

ROLL (SUM OF 2 DICE)	NUMBER OF POSSIBLE COMBINATIONS	PROBABILITY
2	1	3%
3	2	6%
4	3	8%
5	4	11%
6	5	14%
7	6	17%
8	5	14%
9	4	11%
10	3	8%
11	2	6%
12	1	3%

There is no way to roll a one, and that good/bad scenario from the one die example has changed a lot. Rolling a seven with 2 dice has exactly the same probability as rolling any given number with one die, whereas all the other possible rolls have lower probabilities. This is approaching a more normal distribution.

Adding another die will again change the probability of any given outcome. The use of dice is just one way, albeit a common one, to introduce chance and randomness in your game.

Cards can also work very similarly. However, unless a card is directly shuffled back into the deck after being drawn, the probabilities do change, as this card now has a zero percent chance of being drawn. There's also more excitement generally when rolling dice and hoping for the best outcome, so this can impact the feeling of your game as well.

My advice here is to make sure your game is well balanced. That is, ensuring the risk to reward ratio makes sense. This will come with more playtesting along with some understanding of probability.

COMPLEXITY

As you're working on your game, keep the complexity level in mind. This will help determine who the audience will be. If your game involves a lot of complex choices, tricky math, or a lot of strategy, it will likely be geared more towards the hard-core gamer. On the other hand, a game that is very luck-based and simple to play may appeal more to children or families with kids.

The difficulty level of your game may change as you add and remove components, and play around with the theme, in order to align your game with the feeling and experience you're intending. However, if you know what experience you want players to have right off the bat, you should have a relatively good idea of who will be playing your game.

AUDIENCE

There are a number of things you'll want to consider when determining the audience for your game. One of them is the **age range**. You'll want to get a good feel for the youngest players that will be able to grasp the concepts of your game, and whether your game will appeal to both kids and adults.

You may already have an idea of whether your game will be an epic five-hour space quest, or a super quick 10-minute filler game. The **playing time** for a game is important, although many gamers feel that publishers often underestimate this.

The playing time will help determine whether people will be able to play multiple rounds of the game, squeeze it in between other games, or if they need to set aside a good chunk of the day to get through a full play. You'll get a good sense of this as you are playtesting and improving your own game.

You'll also want to consider the **number of players** that your game will allow. Although you might try to be super inclusive by making a game that can be played by anywhere from two to 20 people, you also have to be realistic. You may also be tempted to try to create a game for everyone, but I recommend you narrow your focus. A game for everyone is really a game for no one.

As you're playtesting your game, you'll get a feel for how well it scales to different sized groups. Is your game going to take up a lot of table space? Will all players need to see the board or the card layout at all times? These considerations will also help you to determine how many people can play your game, along with playtesting with various group sizes.

What type of gamer will be interested in your game? Will your game appeal only to hard-core hobbyists? The mass market? Casual gamers?

Maybe it will be geared towards fans of a certain genre or popular movie or series. Just keep Intellectual Property (IP) rights in mind as you are developing your game. You don't want to base a game around an existing license without first obtaining permission.

Maybe there's even a very specific underserved market you're considering. For example, you might find there aren't many really good, engaging religious games available. I'm not saying you have to go out and make one, I'm just trying to get you thinking outside the box (pun intended).

COMPONENTS

As you're working on the first version of your game, it's important to keep it simple. A pen, paper, and scissors may be all you need to get going. Don't worry, this is just a starting point. It's all about getting your first idea to the table quickly.

There are a number of components you'll want to have on hand once you start creating more games (and believe me, more games will be coming!). This doesn't mean you need everything right away, as it highly depends on the game you're creating. Over time though, you will want to have more common components readily available so that you can quickly put together a rough version and test it out.

Here are some other items you may find helpful to have on hand:

- A computer and printer
- Markers
- Card stock (sheets that are a thickness between paper and cardboard)
- Card sleeves
- Dice
- Cards
- Tokens
- Poker chips
- Pennies or other coins
- Figurines/miniatures
- Pawns or meeples
- Cubes or blocks
- Small baggies
- Cloth bags (to draw tiles, dice or other components from)
- Glue, yarn, foam, etc.

Here's a list of places I tend to go to when I need to find components:

- **Dollar Stores** – These are a treasure trove for game designers. You can often find dice, gems, cubes, blocks, stickers, paper supplies, and lots of other neat things for your games.

- **Craft Stores** – While definitely more expensive than some other options, they often have a wide variety of interesting components you can make use of.

- **Old Games** – Look through your own collection and identify any games you no longer play (or just borrow temporarily). Also, make sure to check out thrift stores and garage sales. You can often pick up a game, even one you have no intention of ever playing, for a couple of bucks. Then you can scavenge through them to find many interesting parts.

- **The Gamecrafter and other online game sites** – The Gamecrafter is not only a great place for Print-on-Demand games, but also a fantastic place to pick up some really nice components. They have just about anything you can think of. The prices range from good to high depending on what you want, but you may end up paying a lot for shipping. If you're able to do a group buy with some other designers in your area, you can make it much more cost-effective by ordering together. Search online and see if you can find other similar sites.

You can also check out your Friendly Local Game Store (FLGS) to see if they have anything you need. Note that their prices may be higher than the above options and their selection might be limited compared with online stores.

Whatever components you are using, you'll want to make sure that they are in line with your theme. For example, wooden cubes work well for a resource collecting game, whereas plastic cubes may better suit a space-themed game. However, don't get too caught up on this for the first iteration of your game. There will be plenty of time to find the right components and work on the look of your game later.

WOW FACTOR

With so many games being introduced each year (over 3,500 games funded on Kickstarter alone in 2021 – not to mention other crowdfunding platforms and the larger traditional direct to retail path), there's a lot of competition. How will you make sure that your game stands out?

When competing for shelf space, you'll want to ensure that your game is new and unique. What can you do to make it different from the other games you see out there? What will make people stop when they see others playing your game? What can you do to draw them in?

Now while you'll want your game to be unique, it's often smart to include something familiar. If your game is too "out there" or "off-the-wall," players may not be able to grasp it and you may not be able to get it published. It's often wise to include some elements that are recognizable to players, while at the same time introducing something a little different... something to get their attention.

Here are some examples of games that really stand out:

Santorini – This is a two-player game (well two to four, but it's really best played with two) with really cool looking components. The game is a challenging puzzle, with players stacking up buildings, trying to be the first one to reach the top. When people see this for the first time, they always pause and ask, "Wow, what's that game?" That's the kind of reaction you want to hear!

Scythe - This game by Kickstarter expert and pro designer Jamey Stegmaier, gets a lot of attention through its art and components. This alternative 1920's world was created by artist Jakub Rozalski and implemented into the game. It is a beautiful thing to see set up, with many interesting components and alluring visual style.

Tiny Epic Series – A series of games by Scott Almes that includes *Tiny Epic Defenders, Tiny Epic Galaxies, Tiny Epic Kingdoms,* and others. These tiny games pack a big punch in a small box, laying out an epic adventure without the epic learning time of say the Dungeon Master's Guide (*D&D*).

Ice Cool – Who doesn't love flicking little penguins around?!?!

Fireball Island – Ok, admittedly this game is over 30 years old and maybe isn't the best game out there. Maybe it's just nostalgia, but there's something about the raised island board and rolling fireballs that really grabs your attention! Since the first edition of this book, Restoration Games has also lovingly restored this gem, modernizing the mechanics, and bringing it back to market.

Also, cool, customized miniatures or interesting components can give your game an advantage. Keep in mind however, that anything custom-made adds cost, so you'll want to balance these and other factors when designing your game.

ART AND GRAPHIC DESIGN

Since you're working on a very rough version of your game, you don't want to be spending a lot of time or effort on the art, as this might change, or you may find out that the basic gameplay of your game just doesn't work. Imagine you'd spent 10 hours collecting the perfect art for a game and then found out that you're never going to build it or maybe it's already been invented. What a downer!

What you do want to do is get an idea of the type of art and graphic design you'd like to have in your game. Then find simple ways to include these with little time or effort. These should complement the story, theme, mechanics, and experience you want players to have. Again, just get an idea for what you might want to see in later versions.

USABILITY

When you're designing your game, you'll want to consider the layout, format, and placement of items, art, and icons you use. If you've played a lot of games, especially card games, you'll notice the cards are designed in a specific way. Your eyes naturally go to the top left corner of the card. Conveniently, this is also the area that's displayed when you fan out a hand of cards. You'll want to keep this in mind if your game involves cards, especially if players are holding them.

You'll also want to make sure that any text is easy to read and understand. Make sure your font size is reasonably large, the language is clear, and the colour of the text is contrasted with the background.

Ever notice how commonly certain things appear in games? Remember that you don't have to re-create the wheel. Using something that already works, and players are familiar with is often the best approach to take. Maybe you have a new idea for something that sounds really cool, but if it requires players to think in a different way, you might be better off using what they already know.

You'll also want to consider iconography. What I'm talking about here are the symbols that will be present in your game, if any. If you're creating a resource game, you may need icons for wood, bricks, water, and anything else you might want to include. Make sure that these icons represent the items in a way that is easy for players to understand. Also be consistent throughout the game, trying not to switch up symbols or use something different to mean the same thing.

You also want to acknowledge that some people are colourblind. There are certain colours that some people cannot easily distinguish, such as green and red. I've included a link in the resources section of this book to a helpful site where you can learn more about colourblindness and how to incorporate not only certain colours but also other distinguishable features in your game to make it easier for these players.

Also, it's often useful to have some flavour text on your cards, board, or other components. This gives players a little more background and some interesting things to learn or understand about the game. For example, describe some characteristics about a historical role they are taking on, or explain a bit about an object they've just discovered.

Want to know what helpful resources I use to get my games to the table even faster? Read on and I'll tell you all about them.

ACTION: Determine the win condition for your game, along with the expected difficulty level, age range, number of players, target audience, and components you plan to use for your simple first version. The length of play will be unknown at this time, but you might have an idea of what category it will fall into (short game under 30 minutes, medium length game of 30 to 90 minutes, or a longer game taking over 90 minutes). Also, you'll want to keep in mind for later the usability of various elements in your game, along with what **your** wow factor will be as you are working on this.

SECTION 4

DESIGNING AND PLAYTESTING YOUR GAME

CHAPTER 14
TOOLS AND RESOURCES

"It should be noted that the games of children are not games, and must be considered as their most serious actions."

- Michel de Montaigne, philosopher

There are a lot of tools and resources you can use to create your own board game. You can really go to work, trying to find all sorts of interesting and unique components, but to get started faster, try not to go overboard. In this chapter, I'll cover the basic tools you'll need to get started, and others you may want to add to your collection over time, depending on the types of games you make, and how far along you are with these games.

START WITH THE BASICS

What you need to get started will depend on the type of game you are creating and what components may be necessary. As mentioned, start with the basics. This will likely be a pen, paper, and scissors. Starting with these simple tools, you should be able to get at least a start on your idea, with something rough you can bring to the table and test.

It's handy to have a variety of components you may need for games all together in one place. Rather than having to run around the house trying to find bits and pieces, they will be conveniently available to use as needed.

Don't be afraid to improvise. Use whatever common household items and gaming components you may have laying around. For example:

- Playing cards – if there's anything you need to count in your game, or divide into groups, a deck of playing cards can be really helpful to test out an idea.

- Coins

- Cubes

- Dice

- Parts from other games

- Anything else you can find that is cheap and expendable (hey, stop looking at me!)

Any of the above items can be helpful and may be used in place of tokens, counters, resources, or whatever else you need to get started.

OTHER HELPFUL TOOLS

As you work on your game, you may start to think about other tools that will help you work faster and more efficiently.

For example, you'll likely be cutting out a lot of cards, pieces of paper, card stock, and cardboard, so it may help to have a well-designed paper cutter on hand. Try out the rotary style slider and the guillotine cutter to see which one works better for you. I started with a rotary cutter but I now much prefer my X-Acto guillotine cutter.

It's also helpful to have a box or some kind of organizer for your components. I picked up a storage box years ago after ordering some components online and it was a lifesaver. I've upgraded since then and now have more parts and storage, but this got me through my early days as a game designer very well and I still use it. It helps to keep all my pieces separate from each other, yet it's very easy to reach in and get what I need. My storage box has easy to remove bins for each component, so I don't have to dump everything out when I'm looking for one piece. It also has a handy snap down lid to keep everything in place, and a handle to make it easy to carry.

My component storage solution (closed view)

My first component storage solution (open view)

PRO TIPS

While you want your first version to be very quick and rough just to get your idea to the table to test quickly, once you start developing your game a little further along, it's really helpful to be able to **sleeve your cards**. You can purchase card sleeves from your FLGS, or online at Amazon and other sites.

Have you ever tried to shuffle paper? Not so easy. Sometimes just picking up pieces of paper from the table can be a challenge. Instead, you can slide your own cards into these sleeves, making them easier to handle and shuffle. Also, make sure the cards you print are a little smaller than the sleeves themselves, which makes it much easier to slide the cards in and out.

You can even insert a playing card in behind each one of your cards to make the cards more stable. However, if you're using card stock this may not be necessary. It's up to you. Get a feel for what you like best.

Another cool trick I've seen is to put stickers on coins, such as pennies. This is a cost-effective way to make circular parts that are always identical. You can get a sheet of stickers from the dollar store or from an office supply store. Print out exactly what you need and stick them on either side of the coins. If you put one sticker of the same colour on each side, this can be used to distinguish groups of coins from each other.

Whenever you get the chance, always try to reuse materials. Old prototypes, cardboard boxes, and other things you would otherwise recycle or throw away could come in handy. One person's trash is another person's treasure.

Speaking of group buys, if you're looking for a really large number of items, and know of other people interested in some of the same things, you might want to check out **Alibaba** or other online sites where you can buy large quantities of specific items. Just be aware that the minimum order might be a fairly high quantity. Make sure to check the shipping costs as well!

DON'T LET A LACK OF TOOLS OR RESOURCES HOLD YOU BACK

While it's really great to find that perfect loaf of bread or chicken drumstick component, this isn't at all necessary for trying out your game the first time. Besides, what if your food related game changes themes part way through playtesting and you no longer need those components?

Start with the basics. Use whatever you have on hand to get your game to the table, and fast. No excuses!

Your first version doesn't have to be pretty. In fact, sometimes the uglier, the better! Focus on experience. Test the mechanics to see how they work. Don't spend much time on art – yet. By the time your game is done, you'll want to have beautiful art, design, and components, but that's for when you're nearing completion. Just keep it simple to start, then you can start building in all the art and components you want as your game nears completion.

Next up, I'll show you how to get that idea out of your head and onto the table in no time!

ACTION: Find a box or other storage solution. Now walk around your house and find things you need to get started, including paper, pens, scissors, and anything else that may be helpful. Don't take a lot of time with this. Just get the basics to get you going.

If you really think there's something you can't do without before you get started, take a quick trip to the dollar store and do some hunting. Put all your components into your game design box, using separators or small containers to keep everything organized. You're now ready to start playing your game!

CHAPTER 15
MINIMUM VIABLE PROTOTYPE (MVP)

"However it happens, many games I design, and I would wager many you have and will design, start from humble, scrappy beginnings and require a lot of experimentation and support to be ready for prime time."

– Teale Fristoe, contributor on League of Game Makers

There is a great concept in the business world that applies really well to board game design. This concept is the Minimum Viable Prototype, or MVP. This is adapted from the term "Minimum Viable Product." Creating your MVP means that rather than develop a product fully before knowing if there is any demand or interest in it, you put together the simplest possible version to test the idea first. This can save you a lot of time and effort.

GETTING YOUR IDEA TO THE TABLE QUICKLY

Getting an idea out of your head and onto the table as quickly as possible is a crucial step. It allows you to have "something" to work with. This is the starting point from which you can move forward. You can work from this early version and continue to make improvements to it, or know very quickly that it won't work.

The point is to turn this from a thought into something tangible. After putting this on paper, it will likely look and play very differently than you imagined. There's your game in theory, and then there's your game in reality. Just don't let that idea get stuck in your head. You have to transform it into something you can play around with.

Your first version is going to be very basic. You're going to be working mainly with pen, paper and scissors, along with any other minimal components you may need to test out your first version. Remember, this is just an idea you're testing out at this point.

I have seen and heard stories of some very rough ideas that were merely sketches on the backs of cards, or just a concept thrown together and discussed amongst a few designers, that evolved into something special really quickly. I've been known to whip up just a small number of topic cards or trivia questions for a game idea, knowing full well the complete version of the game would require hundreds of these. Why would I want to spend the time and energy to create a full box of cards before I know whether the concept will even work?

It's best to try with a small sample, and see if there really is something to your idea first. My friend, Chris Chung, once commented to me at a game designer night that he was really happy with what he thought was about 25% of an idea that he brought to the table. He hashed this out with a few other designers, and lo and behold, less than an hour later he had a really solid foundation to start from.

YOU'RE ONLY TESTING A CONCEPT AT THIS POINT

When you're putting together your MVP, you're really trying to answer the question "does this idea work?" You're trying to get a feel for whether the mechanics you thought of applying will fit. You're also checking to see whether your idea conveys the experience you are intending for players.

YOUR FIRST VERSION WILL BE TERRIBLE

Okay. I said it. It's true. Your first version **will** be terrible. At least chances are it will be. The good news is that's ok. This is totally normal. Almost every designer has said the same thing about most of their initial ideas. This certainly was the case with my first game.

Don't let this slow you down or hold you back. Remember that even the most seasoned game designer doesn't come to the table with an unblemished initial idea.

Nobody's perfect. And no new product or idea (board game or otherwise), works completely as intended the first time. You know where WD-40 (the lubricant) got its name? It was the 40th version of the product they tested before they got it right. It could've easily been called WD-87 had they not nailed it earlier.

YOU NEVER FORGET YOUR FIRST

The first game I created was a party game called *Cunning Linguistics*. After I had been playing some party games repeatedly with friends, the idea came to me to make something similar, but with much more creativity and replayability. It felt so perfect in my head. But when I created the cards and tried it out with friends, it completely fell apart. It was hard to create answers with the words I had provided, the distribution of words was all wrong, and the way I had laid it all out was excessively slow and clunky.

Fortunately, I could tell that there was a solid and pretty funny idea here; I just had to figure out the best way to put it all together. Just trying out my idea allowed me to see what worked and what didn't, and what I could possibly try next. Over time, the game has become something really fun, and I get requests to play it. What would happen if I gave up after that first playtest? I never would have created my first game, gone on to design a bunch more, and I definitely couldn't have written this book!

I also had an idea for a card game related to "playing chicken," but I didn't know whether the concept would work. So, I simply took a deck of playing cards, set aside the face cards, and tried the idea by myself. It wasn't super fun right off the bat, but thought it had some potential. So, I tried this with my wife. This next playtest went a whole different direction.

She ended up using the same strategy every time, winning each hand, and we both realized quickly that it was the optimal strategy. This gave me more to think about, and I understood that the game would need additional goals and restrictions. It only took me a few minutes to try out this initial concept, and it was extremely useful in helping me understand what I had to do next.

As I mentioned, your game will likely change a lot over the course of playtesting. You're going to be constantly trying new ideas and approaches, with the goal of always moving your game forward. Your approach will be to make little changes, see if it improves, and make it a better player experience with each version, one that is in harmony with your vision.

Ok, we've covered a lot. You've got your idea. You have your MVP put together. Now, let's play!

ACTION: Put together a Minimum Viable Prototype (MVP) for your game idea. Spend no more than five to ten minutes on gathering components, jotting things down on cards, or creating any rough parts to try out your game for the first time.

CHAPTER 16
HOW TO RUN YOUR FIRST PLAYTEST

"Game design is an iterative process. It's all about failure, watching how the game doesn't work, and learning from it. That usually involves sweating over a new tweak, figuring out how to implement it, printing and slicing all the components, and then getting it to the table and watching it completely throw the game off-balance in a new direction."

– Gil Hova, designer of The Networks

You've come up with an amazing game concept. You've gathered all the materials you need and have put together a very rough prototype. Now it's time to try out your idea by running your first playtest.

START WITH YOUR GOAL IN MIND

Whenever you conduct a playtest, you're really just testing a hypothesis. You're trying to figure out if something will work. Simply put, in the first playtest of your game, the goal is always to find out "does this work?" You'll be trying out simple concepts, interested to see whether they work, or if the game "breaks" (i.e., something doesn't work properly or the way you had imagined it). You want to find out whether it is awkward, smooth, slow, tedious, or otherwise.

One of the big questions to ask is whether the mechanics work. You've thought out everything in your head, and it works perfectly there. Now, does it work in reality?

Although you're at a very early stage, you still want to be thinking about what initial feelings you have when playing your game. Do these feelings match your vision? Are they different? Are they interesting? Maybe they're unexpected. As I mentioned, it's still early, but you'll want to keep these types of questions in mind.

Every time you create a board game you will go through a continuous four-step cycle that I refer to as **The 4 I's Framework:**

1. **Inquire** through playtesting

2. **Identify** any problems

3. **Illuminate** potential solutions

4. **Iterate** and revise your game

INQUIRE
through playtesting

ITERATE
and revise
your game

IDENTIFY
any problems

ILLUMINATE
potential solutions

First you must **inquire**. By this, I am referring to running your playtest and observing the results.

Next, **identify any problems** by asking your playtesters for feedback. Determine what didn't work and what aspects of your game could have been improved. Remember, we're looking to first **identify** problems rather than solutions. This is a key distinction.

Third, you will try to **illuminate potential solutions** by brainstorming a number of ideas, either by yourself or with the help of the other designers or playtesters.

Fourth, you will **iterate**. By this, I mean that you will select the best option from these potential solutions to test and make a revision to your game, which you will then playtest again.

Once you have created your MVP, you can begin to use this framework. You will be using this process and feedback cycle continuously until you feel your game is as complete as it can be.

At times you will be running through this framework over and over while running through a single playtest, and other times you will be gathering this feedback and making changes at a later time. I'll show you exactly how to apply this framework over the next few chapters. So, without further ado, let's start playtesting!

START OUT SOLO OR WITH ONE OTHER PERSON

If possible, first just get your rough draft to the table by yourself, and see how the game plays out. Did it work as it did in your head? What's different? Look at both the good and bad. Obviously, it could be very difficult to play a full game by yourself, but by acting out the actions that players would take in your game, it will give you a feel of whether or not the concept will even work as you had thought.

Once you've had a look at it by yourself (unless it wouldn't make any sense to do so by yourself), ask a partner, close friend, or family member if you can try out your idea with him or her. If it is a game that will absolutely require more people, such as one that involves trading, voting, or deduction, you may need a slightly larger group, but do try to play out some scenarios by yourself or with one other person at first if possible.

Make sure to let anyone you're playtesting with know that the objective at first, like the name implies, is simply to test the idea. Let them know you're trying to figure out if this idea will even work.

Most people are used to, and may be more interested in, playing complete, published games, so the idea of playtesting a very rough prototype may be unusual to them. If this is their first time playtesting a game, guide them through what you're thinking of, and what you're trying to test. You'll be following the **4 I's Framework** throughout to identify and resolve any issues as you go.

But what if you live in a remote place, or don't have anyone interested in playtesting your game with you? Or maybe you just want to get this going right away and don't want to wait to get an event organized. Well, the great news is there are some helpful simulation programs that you can use to test out your game anytime online.

Two common simulators are **Tabletop Simulator** (TTS) and **Tabletopia**, both of which are available online. Tabletopia is free for up to one prototype and is browser-based, while Tabletop Simulator is a paid app, however many feel that Tabletop Simulator is better since it is much easier to use. Tabletop Playground is a newer platform, similar to TTS as well.

There are many online communities for playtesting, so if you go this route, you could playtest your game practically every day of the week with other game designers from around the world.

It can be really fun to use any of these platforms to create a prototype and this allows you to very easily make changes on the fly without having to cut cards, reprint pages, or find new components. However, you can also very easily get sucked into spending a lot of time here perfecting your game with all the options so easily available. If you choose to make use of an online game simulator, I caution you to just get a simple working version going before spending a lot of time figuring out art and design, and "prettying up" your game.

TESTING YOUR IDEA

At this point, what you're doing is really testing your "proof of concept." By that, I mean whether the idea you have in your head actually works. Remember, it's still just an idea. You're trying to piece together what makes your concept an interesting game, along with what themes and mechanics would help enhance this.

Your first question is whether your game concept is fun and worth pursuing.

I'll let you know right now that your first version and first playtest will not go that smoothly. Things won't work exactly as you had imagined, and it may be no fun at all. My first playtest was terrible. But that didn't stop me. Don't give up.

Keep in mind that this is only a very rough first version of what your game will eventually become. It's going to take time, but your game will keep getting better. Keep following the steps outlined in this book, and you'll do just fine. I will walk you through what to do next, and how to keep improving your game, ensuring that it will become something really special. Just hang in there!

Don't be afraid to try something different with your game. Even if it seems crazy. Some of the craziest ideas can lead to something really unique and interesting.

SWITCH ON THE FLY

You'll also want to let your fellow playtesters know that you may want to make changes on the fly as issues are discovered and new ideas are brought forward. You'll want to make sure they are comfortable with this, as they may not be used to stopping and starting, or changing rules during the course of a game.

Iteration is what it's all about. You want to fail quickly. Be prepared and learn how to embrace failure. You'll have many more failures and successes, but each one will bring you one step closer all the time. It may be hard at first, but you will get used to this and be able to treat failure not as a setback, but as an opportunity to identify and solve a problem, in order to make your game that much better.

Many of your playtests, especially those at the very beginning, will involve a lot of "how about this?", or "let's try that." You'll get the chance to figure out what's working and what isn't. If something is not working, you can brainstorm some ways to get around the issue, and try something that may allow it to run better. Just keep following the **4 I's Framework**.

LETTING GO

Don't let yourself be tied to one idea. I've heard plenty of stories from professional designers about a mechanic they absolutely loved and tried to introduce into new games. Quite often, it was the basis for the original game idea, and everything revolved around this. But after many playtests, it became evident that the mechanic was not really necessary, and in fact may have been holding the game back.

Although it may be difficult, sometimes you have to let go of an idea that just isn't working, even if it was once the core mechanic in your game. You can always keep note of this mechanic or theme in your notebook, and try to use it somewhere else where it might work better. This may just evolve into a whole new game.

When an issue arises, you'll also want to brainstorm a number of possible solutions to try to resolve it. Don't necessarily go with the first idea that comes to mind or initial suggestion that's presented. There are usually a number of possible solutions to a problem. Generate some ideas, and test whichever one you think is the most feasible or interesting. If it works well, great! If not go back to your notes and try something else.

I mentioned earlier my idea for a game of "playing chicken" that didn't work out on the first playtest. That initial test allowed me to see right away that my first version was broken. So, I brainstormed a number of possible ideas to get around it. This included changing the number and point value of cards, creating a different point structure, adding additional goals, creating disincentives and roadblocks, and adding in a random player. This gave me plenty of options, which allowed me to choose the most feasible one, test, and move on.

It may be difficult, but sometimes you do have to let a game die. You'll have lots of ideas, and some of them will be great, but others just won't work. They may turn into a functional game, but they may not be any fun. If a game just isn't getting better and it isn't providing the experience you want for people, you may be better off putting this on the shelf, either until a later time, or for good.

After your initial playtests, you'll have a game that is starting to come together. Now it's time to share this with others to make it even better! Keep reading and I'll show you how.

If you're looking for more of a personal touch and want even more help with your game, check out the Board Game Design Course boardgame-designcourse.com. The course includes access to a community of game designer just like you, along with group Q&A coaching calls with Joe.

ACTION: Lay out the first version of your game and trial it by yourself or with another person (or a few people if necessary). Try out the actions you have in your head and see how it goes. Does the game work? If it does, try it out with another person and see if this still holds up. If not, use the **4 I's Framework** to first trial your game (**inquiry**), figure out what's not working (**identify the problem**), brainstorm some possible solutions (**illuminate potential solutions**), pick one idea to try, make changes (**iterate**) and test this out again (back to **inquiry** again). Repeat as necessary, then try it out with someone else when you feel you're ready.

CHAPTER 17
ONGOING PLAYTESTS

"If I'm not truly open to changing my mind, it means that I'm also probably not listening to people who have different opinions, which severely limits my potential for growth and improvement."

– Jamey Stegmaier, Kickstarter expert and creator of Scythe

Now that you've playtested your game at least a few times, and feel that the basic concepts are working, it's time to take your playtesting to the next level.

CONTINUE TESTING YOUR GAME WITH FRIENDS AND FAMILY

You now have a better understanding of playtesting, and you'll want to do more of this with friends, family members, or coworkers. Again, you'll be testing assumptions. You have a better feeling for your game and how it works, there will be other specific goals you'll have for your next play-tests. You'll want to see how it plays with more people and different groups as well.

Once again, start with your goal in mind. You'll want to be very clear about what you are testing with each new version of your game. Make sure to let those who are playtesting with you know exactly what type of feedback you are looking for. You don't have to just sit back though, you can play along with them if you choose.

You'll also want to address the fact that your art and design is very rough at this point, and that this isn't your focus right now. Rather, you're trying to figure out something specific, such as whether having five options for cards to choose from on the table as opposed to three will make the game better.

Remember also that you can stop or pause your playtest at any time if something's not working. You don't always have to test the entire game from start to finish. You also don't want to make people suffer through a really brutal playtest if something isn't quite right, as they'll be less likely to want to playtest for you in the future.

Respect their time, and get a feel for whether they're enjoying the game or are frustrated by some aspect of it. I was at a game designer night once and another designer was setting up his game. He recruited some play-testers and they asked how long the game took. His response was "four hours." However, he let them know right away that he only playtests for two rounds, which takes roughly one hour.

This is really good for players to know before starting. Many people would be turned off by a four hour plus playtest, especially if the game is still pretty rough. Speaking of time, make sure to time your playtest to get a good feel for the length of your game and how it varies (by player count and otherwise) if you are running your playtest through from start to finish.

Follow the **4 I's Framework**. Make sure to take lots of notes. You want to capture the reactions that people have along with their interest in the game. Are players engaged or distracted? Body language can often speak louder than words. If people are checking their phones more than playing your game, then you might have a problem!

Also, understand what issues people are having as they play. Are the rules unclear? Is something too complex? Does something just not make sense?

As people play your game, you'll start to think about things that you may want to try next. You'll want to have all this written down. Also, compare the player count to what you had imagined. Does this match well? Are there any issues with scaling it up or down?

Maybe your game plays really well with two players, but when you try it with four, it slows down to a snail's pace. These are valuable pieces of information you'll want to remember.

BE SPECIFIC

At the end of your playtest, make sure to ask specific questions. A question such as "did you like it?" doesn't give you much to work with. It's too vague. Players will generally tell you whether they liked it or not. Then again, knowing you're the designer, they may not want to hurt your feelings if they weren't a big fan.

You're trying to figure out what people like best about game and what they disliked so that you can improve it and make it as good as possible.

So, make sure to ask specific questions about your playtest. One of the best suggestions I've heard came from prolific game designer Sen-Foong Lim, who suggests asking "If you played this game again, and just **one** thing was different that made you think the game had improved, **even only by 5%**... what would be different?" This is a great question to pose in order to understand the biggest pain point that players had with your game.

You may also want to ask about and understand the main feeling that players had while playing your game. Does it match what you had intended? If you are testing a specific mechanic, ask how they felt about this. Or, if they have tried your game previously when it was using a different mechanic, ask them to comment on which version they preferred, and why.

One other question I love to pose to the winning player is whether they felt they earned the win. I want to avoid players feeling they won completely by luck. On the flipside, I like to ask others if they felt like they were still in the game, as you don't want players feeling like they had no chance to win by a few turns in and were just going though the motions. That's never a fun experience.

It can also be helpful to ask players how long they thought they had been playing. If it is around the same or less than the actual time, that's probably an indication that time flew by and they were enjoying the experience. You can also ask generally if the game felt too long, too short, or just about right. You don't want your game to overstay its welcome, but it can be good for players to feel like they wanted even more.

Once you've identified the main issues players have (along with some possible solutions that will inevitably be thrown your way), it's time for you to brainstorm solutions again.

You'll then decide which one you want to try next and playtest it again to determine whether it improved the game, worsened it, or simply made it different. You'll be following the **4 I's Framework** with each playtest.

Make sure to not only test with one group, because they will end up getting very familiar with the game. They will recognize how it's improved, understand strategies fairly well, and provide very different feedback from a group seeing your game for the first time. Remember that down the road when somebody buys your game, they will be playing this for the first time. What experience will they have? New groups will also offer new perspectives and may uncover issues that others did not see.

GETTING UNBIASED FEEDBACK

Playing your new game with friends and family can be a lot of fun, but you need to recognize that the feedback you get from people who know and love you may be very different from the feedback you'll get from strangers. You want to know what others who might be interested in your game think about it, because they could ultimately be your customers. The next step is to repeat the same process, but with people you **don't** know. This may include other board game designers, playtesters, and board game fans.

I know. It's sometimes hard enough to get your friends and loved ones together to try out your game. And they know and love you! You're probably asking yourself "how in the world am I going to get people I **don't know** to play my game?"

Fortunately, there are more options available than ever before. It's not only a great time to be a board game enthusiast, but it's also a great time to be a board game designer. I'm going to walk you through a number of different choices you have for getting your game playtested by strangers, which in turn will also get you more involved in the board game community, which is always a great thing!

PLAYTESTING/PROTOTYPING EVENTS AND PROTOSPIELS

There are lots of these prototyping events going on, but there may or may not be any happening in your area. Depending on where you live and where these events are, this may involve some travel.

However, these events are typically filled with many game designers, who are often the best people to provide you with feedback on your game. They've been there. Board game designers are amazing and always willing to share their experiences. Look for upcoming events and try to attend one (or more) if possible.

GAME DESIGNER NIGHTS AND EVENTS

If you have any FLGS or board game cafés nearby, there's a good chance that they will offer a game designer night, maybe as frequently as once or twice per month. If they don't, ask them about setting one up. This is a great opportunity for them to bring people in on a night that is otherwise quiet, which can help them do more business, while allowing the local game design community to thrive.

Other game designers may also hold events where they live, or at nearby community centres or other locations. Look around to see what's happening in and around your city or town.

BOARD GAME CONVENTIONS

Board Game Conventions or "Cons" as they are affectionately called, range in size from small local get-togethers to giant meet-ups with over 100,000 attendees, such as Gen Con and Essen. With this wide variety comes varied opportunities. The small Cons may just involve people getting together to play games, whereas larger Cons may offer plenty of opportunities to playtest your game with willing participants as well as discuss your game with publishers.

Check out what's happening close to home as well as at the larger conventions. Every Con is filled with gaming fans, and may be an opportunity to get some good feedback from people who don't know you.

BOARD GAME GROUPS

There may be meetups and board game groups in your area. You'll want to check them out and join in if they are available. If not, why not start your own? Look for others who are interested in playing and/or designing games and create a meetup of your own. It may start out small but could grow over time. Look around to try to find other local board game designers, playtesters, and board game fans. You may be able to attract a small but loyal following.

ONLINE PLAYTESTING

It may just be the case that you live somewhere remote or can't find a group of board gamers in your area. Or maybe your schedule just won't allow it. As mentioned previously, there are some good board game simulators available, where you can create your own game and allow others to try it out. You can playtest your game here with someone you don't know, and get real-time feedback.

As mentioned, Tabletop Simulator and Tabletopia are two well-known platforms for this very purpose. Screentop.gg, Playingcards.io, and Tabletop Playground are other alternatives. Keep your eyes open for new options and groups that may be available as well.

PLAYTEST FOR OTHERS

Don't forget about the power of reciprocity. Ask others if you can help them by playtesting their game. People have a tendency to want to pay back favours rather than be in debt to someone, and they will often repay the original person back and then some. Remember, the more you give, the more you get.

CRITIQUING FEEDBACK

When you ask for feedback, you're going to get it, whether it's positive or negative. You want to encourage people to be truthful because otherwise your game won't continuously improve and reach its full potential. However, I know it's not always easy to take critical feedback.

Remember that feedback is meant to be helpful and improve your game. Don't take it personally. Whether the feedback is good, bad, or ugly, you want to make sure to thank that person, and show appreciation for them taking the time to play your game and give their thoughts.

Don't immediately jump to the defensive. Of course, there's a reason why you did things a certain way in your game, but you don't have to defend every single one of them. If someone suggests something you've already tried, let them know that it's a great idea, and in fact you did try it, and explain what happened when you did.

Your game is just an idea, which will change and evolve over time. Don't get too tied to any one thing. If a suggestion from a player is unclear, ask for clarification. If someone suggests something you know will absolutely not work, or will go completely against the player experience you are trying to attain, ask them to go into greater detail and explain exactly how that revision might work. They may find that by talking it out it will become clear that the suggestion won't actually fix the problem, or perhaps they **will** come up with something great that you can use.

You'll receive all types of feedback, from all types of people. You'll want to consider issues that are brought up by multiple people more than you would one-off comments generally. If everyone is telling you that the turns take too long, then they probably are. That's something you'll want to fix. But if one guy makes an obscure complaint that no one else has, it may not be worth further thought.

YOU GET BETTER WITH EXPERIENCE

The best way to understand what feedback is helpful and what's not is through experience. The more playtests you do, and the more feedback you get, the quicker you will be able to weed out the useful from the not so useful.

As always, you'll be following the **4 I's Framework**. What you are really doing by playtesting is identifying problems. This is the main goal. You'll uncover issues, then brainstorm and problem solve. Guide your playtesters to help you identify the problems, and do your best to follow this advice as well when you're playtesting for others.

The reality is that people often jump to solutions. Rather than identifying the problem, they will start throwing out suggestions like "we should have more cards," or "can we roll dice to attack?", when all you really want to know is what the issue is.

Maybe the players feel like they don't have enough choice, or something is too luck-based. You want to be a problem identifier first, and problem solver second. Now, that isn't to say you won't get some good ideas from players, especially from experienced designers, however it's ultimately your call, because it's your game.

IDENTIFY THE PROBLEM FIRST

If you focus on getting players to identify problems rather than solutions right off the bat, you can also avoid a player trying your game again at a later date and complaining how you didn't include one of their suggestions. It's much better to have them understand and identify what the problem was, so that they can later comment on how much better the game flows or how well a certain problem was fixed.

You may get some people throwing out a plethora of suggestions. They may rattle off 18 different things you can try, without getting to the root of the problem. You'll want to watch for this, as it may be the case of someone imposing their own vision on your game. Guide them back to identifying the problem, and remember that you have the final say.

Others may not have much to say. You might get a simple "I liked it," or "I didn't like it." This isn't all that helpful, to say the least. Try to get them to dive deeper. Ask them what they liked or didn't like about the game, and go back to Sen's question about the one thing that they would change next time they play the game.

You may also run into the case of somebody intentionally trying to "break" your game. It may seem strange, but some people take pleasure in trying to find a way to make your game not work as intended. However, this can actually be helpful, as it may unearth issues with your game you wouldn't have otherwise found. This player may try "weird" strategies or take the same actions over and over, which may not make sense, but nonetheless can be done. Make sure to take note whenever your game breaks and how this has been accomplished.

If you're playtesting your game with other board game designers, you may also notice that some will make suggestions along the lines of what they would like to see and how they would design the game. While you may get some great ideas, remember that everyone has their biases and you have the ultimate say in what direction your game goes.

It's also important to take downtime into account. How much time do players have to wait until their next turn? Is there anything they can do while other people are playing (strategizing, interacting with the active player, etc.)? It's good to aim for keeping turns short or simultaneous. Rather than having one player complete five different actions, you may want to try having each player complete one action and move on to the next player to increase engagement.

If you notice a player is uninterested during the play, don't be afraid to ask why. Maybe they find it too slow. Maybe they're bored waiting for their turn. Perhaps they're just not finding the game engaging and have lost interest. Identify the issue and brainstorm ideas for how to fix this. Try to make sure this is solved in your next version. Now let's get into how to do this all even faster!

Action: Playtest your game with people you don't know. Find out what groups and events are available in your area or consider using an online board game simulator. Then test your game with as many groups as you can, making iterations and improvements with every version. Make sure at the end of each playtest to ask specific, helpful questions to get the best feedback you can.

CHAPTER 18
ITERATE QUICKLY (TEST, TEST, TEST!)

"Anyone can make the simple complicated. Creativity is making the complicated simple."

- Charles Mingus, jazz pianist

In this chapter, I'm going to walk you through the steps to take feedback, make improvements to your game, playtest, and repeat, in a manner that will allow you to iterate quickly and move closer and closer to finishing your game.

HOW LONG WILL IT TAKE TO FINISH MY GAME?

You might be starting to wonder just how much time it will take to complete your game. The honest answer, which applies to a lot of questions is, it depends. Are you creating a simple party game? An epic legacy game? These could have vastly different timelines. "Finished" is also a tricky term, as you could continue to work on a game forever, and even though you may feel you've done everything you can with your game, a publisher (if your game is picked up by one) will almost always continue to make changes.

To put things in perspective, the hugely successful game *Scythe* took Jamey Stegmaier about 14 months to create from start to finish, working on it full-time. The legacy games that Rob Daviau makes can take a year or two to complete. Many first-time designers may take years trying to perfect their game working on it off and on (you shouldn't aim for perfect though!).

On the other hand, I've heard that Vlaada Chvatil created *Codenames* in about an hour. It probably took at little more time to finalize everything, but the basic concept came together in no time. Granted, Vlaada has made a ton of more complex games, and as an experienced designer this came together for him much more quickly than it would have if it were his first design.

You can work on your game for as long or as short of a time as you choose. Of course, the more you work on it, and work on it consistently, the better it will get. To an extent. You don't want to work on it forever. If your game isn't overly complex, and you work on it routinely following the steps outlined in this book, there's a very good chance that your game will be nearing the final stages within 6-12 months, however, don't be surprised if your game takes longer than this. Many great games have taken years to develop (note that this doesn't mean the designer has worked on it every day though).

MAKING YOUR GAME BETTER VERSUS MAKING IT DIFFERENT

When running your playtests, you're going to get all sorts of feedback. You need to be able to distinguish what feedback will help make your game better as opposed to just making it different.

I'd love to give you a magic formula or be able to tell you exactly what feedback will be most helpful, but this is something that differs with every game and playtest, so you'll have to discover this through experience. The good news is, the more you playtest, the better you'll be able to distinguish what's helpful from what's not.

The feedback you receive can lead you down so many paths of possibility. However, it can be very time-consuming and not so feasible to try every possible approach that's suggested. What you want to do is focus on the ideas that will really help you improve your game. But how do you accomplish this?

One way to do this is focus on the most fun part of your game. Whether it involves backstabbing other players, building a powerful engine, using superpowers, or whatever it might be, see if you can focus the game around this, and add more of this element.

Consequently, you may want to have less of other things in your game that aren't quite as much fun. You may end up dropping some mechanics or aspects of the game, even the ones that you love and were originally the heart of the game. If it's just not a fun part of the game, it may be worth making this change.

Also look to see if there are ways to get to the fun part of your game faster. If there is a long lead-up or build to get to the fun part, maybe you can find a way to let the players start further along, bypassing some of the slower or less interesting initial steps. Rather than have players take a long, winding journey to the enchanted cave, why not start them out at the entrance and get them right into the heart of the action?

You'll also want to balance fun vs. realism. While you want your game to be thematic, make sense, and follow a story, you may need to sacrifice some reality to make the game more fun. If there's any part of the game or story that's tedious or slow, you may want to remove these parts.

For example, if you're making a game about racing, pit stops would be a natural part of this. However, if this slows down your game or takes away from the fun, you may want to consider eliminating this aspect.

TRY DIFFERENT THINGS

If something isn't quite working right in your game, you may want to change things up. This includes the mechanics. Even if the mechanic was at the core of your game initially, that doesn't mean that it will survive into the final version. Remember, everything except your vision and intended player experience are fair game.

And don't forget, you can always take a step back if something doesn't work. When I was working on *Isle of Rock and Roll*, my game about forming a rock band and competing with other bands on stage, I received what was a great sounding suggestion during a playtest, so I made that change immediately. I brought the game back to the event the next day to try it out with this awesome revision, and it completely flopped. What sounded good in theory did not work in practice. But I wouldn't have known this if I didn't try. No sweat though, I just reverted back to the previous version and continued to playtest and make changes from there.

You also shouldn't worry about solidifying the rules yet. Definitely make notes about what players are allowed to do on their turns, and other things to keep in mind, but at this point you want to remain flexible. Don't set your rules in stone. Continue to make changes as your game progresses. Update your rough draft rules with what's working, and strike out what's not.

SIMPLIFY

When in doubt, you're almost always better off removing something than adding something to your game. This is usually the more effective approach. Figure out what's not working, and what is not enhancing the experience, and consider removing this from your game. Run another playtest and see if this works better. If not, as I mentioned you can always revert back to your previous version.

If your game becomes too complex, players may tune out. You want them to feel challenged and have some interesting and sometimes tough decisions, but you don't want to have so much going on that they become confused or completely lose interest. Generally, one new mechanic per game is plenty. More than that can make a game overwhelming to learn.

CHANGE ONE THING AT A TIME

By changing one aspect of your game at a time, you'll quickly be able to tell if that change improved your game. Conversely, if you change a bunch of things at once, you won't know what helped or hindered.

However, in the early stages, your game is still finding its footing. So, complete overhauls are sometimes necessary in the early going.

TRACK PROGRESS

I've mentioned that you should always be creating. Always be testing. But you also need to always be taking notes. You want to record the results of your playtests, issues that have arisen, ideas for changes you want to try, and anything else that will be helpful for the next iteration. Always make sure to document your next steps on a game. This makes it way easier to come back the next time you pick this up off the shelf.

Do not rely on your memory. You may not remember specific comments, or worse yet, you remember them incorrectly. By documenting your next step, you can get right back into testing and making changes, without any time wasted. I strongly suggest you do this for all your games, especially later on if you have multiple games on the go, as this will be a life saver.

Make sure to note what worked and what didn't. If something's not working, this will be the next thing you'll want to revise. Also, make sure to celebrate what is working, and see if there are opportunities to implement more of this in your game.

Once again, you will be coming back to the player experience and feeling. How did players react while playing your game? Was their experience in line with your expectations? What elements of the game really enhanced the player experience? What elements took away from this experience? The answers to these questions will help guide you as you work on the next version of your game.

It's also important to record the scores from each game. This will give you some great information to use later on. For example, were the scores fairly close? Was everyone in the running and did everyone feel they still had a chance to win? If not, you may see players become disengaged, as they feel they have no hope of winning and their actions won't matter.

It's also interesting to know whether there was a runaway leader. If your game allows this to happen, you may need to consider a catch-up or rubber band mechanisms that will allow players near the back the chance to catch up or at least be competitive.

Recording scores, particularly in the order that players played, if applicable, can also be helpful in identifying whether any players have an advantage. For example, in some games you may find that the first player wins much more often than other players. If after a number of playtests you notice a trend, you may want to put something in place to decrease or eliminate any real or perceived advantage that one particular player has.

ADDING ART AND GRAPHIC DESIGN

While I encourage you to make the first version of your game very simplistic, and not focus on the appearance too much, you will want to start implementing more art and design into your game as you get closer to a final version. This will make your game more visually appealing, which has some advantages, and can really add to the experience. Remember however, that this art is temporary. Do not spend a lot of time on it and definitely **don't spend any money** on art and graphic design at this point. It's just too early, and besides, depending on the route you take, this may change dramatically by the time your game is done.

What you want at this point are free images. Google Images are a good starting point and you can certainly find a lot there. Just be aware that most of these images are not necessarily royalty free, so you will not be able to use them in your final version. Likewise, Clipart can be used, however this will likely not be super high quality. There are lots of websites with royalty-free images, photos, and icons that can be used as well.

As you move away from pen and paper, and start utilizing your computer to design cards and other parts of your game, you'll want to use software that you find comfortable and effective. This can vary considerably from one person to another. If you are very familiar with graphic design or photography, you may consider using Photoshop, InDesign, or other similar programs. Some people may prefer to use programs like Word, Excel, and PowerPoint, which they may already own.

I'd also like to introduce you to a really good online solution called Canva. I find this to be an extremely easy to use and helpful design program. It's free, user-friendly, and is filled with lots of templates, fonts, and symbols that you can start using right away.

If you're looking at automating some of your processes and avoiding re-work, it's worth looking into NanDeck, Component Studio or Card Creator. These programs will allow you to make one update in a spreadsheet and have this applied to any or all of the cards in a deck. So, rather than changing that one icon manually on 100 different cards, you can do this once with one quick change.

I've also heard good things about Inkscape and GIMP, however I haven't used these yet myself. Check out the links to all of these in the resource section of this book.

The final art and graphic design are up to the publisher. They will have the final call, so unless you know for sure that you will be self-publishing your game, don't spend any money on art and graphic design.

You just want to make sure that the art matches what you want players to experience and that the graphic design is intuitive. Ask playtesters if symbols and their placement make sense or if anything is confusing. It's all about making sure that players can understand what is happening in your game and interpret rules and symbols correctly.

After all these playtests and iterations, you will soon be able to envision your game sitting on the shelf of your local game store beside all the other games that you love. You'll be in the home stretch once you complete the final and ultimate phase of playtesting, but first, we'll want to make sure players understand how to play your game.

ACTION: Continue playtesting and making improvements to your game, and make sure to track the progress you're making all the way through. Your game will be getting better all the time. Continue this cycle by using the **4 I's Framework** until you feel like your game plays well consistently, with an engaging experience that matches the feeling you want players to have.

CHAPTER 19
FINALIZING YOUR RULES

"You have to learn the rules of the game. And then you have to play better than anyone else."

– Albert Einstein

Once you've run a number of playtests and feel your game is getting pretty close to being finalized, you'll want to ensure you have some well-documented and laid out rules. In order to create an effective set of rules, we must first understand what rules are used for. The main purpose of rules are to **learn a game** and to **refer back/refresh your memory**.

Rules are often considered the bane of a game designer's existence. But have no fear. Follow the simple steps I outline ahead, and players will understand your game as if it was their own.

HOW TO WRITE A GOOD RULE BOOK

Three aspects that are critical to a good set of rules include ensuring they are **easy to follow**, include **helpful visuals**, and that they walk players through the **proper steps in order**.

EASY TO FOLLOW

By easy to follow, I mean that the rules should use simple, consistent language, symbols, and terms. They should be easy to understand and laid out in a logical manner.

You'll want to make sure your language is clear throughout your rules. Do your best to use common language and terms. If you are introducing new terminology based on an original theme, make sure to explain everything clearly.

Make sure that everything is in the correct order as well. Rather than have players jump back and forth between rules, make sure that the flow is smooth and in the order that players will encounter throughout the game.

Be sure to use the same terminology throughout your rules. For example, if you have a game that takes place in a restaurant and players are taking on the roles of chefs, always refer to them as "chefs," never as "cooks." Likewise, either use the term "cubes," or "blocks," but not both of these words to refer to the same thing. Make sure to be clear about terms like round, turn, and action, so that players understand clearly what happens when.

Players should be able to find the right information in the right place at the right time. They shouldn't have to wade through pages of rules to find something because it is not in a logical location. Make things easy to find. If necessary, repeat crucial pieces of information, but make sure not to overdo it. You don't want your rules to be too repetitive.

HELPFUL VISUALS

It's also important to include helpful visuals in your rules, to ensure players understand what the game should look like when it is set up, and what players can and cannot do. Many people learn visually, so it's important to not only include text, but also visuals and examples to help people walk through the setup, actions, and any other important aspects of your game.

In your rulebook, it's often very helpful to document the moves that players are allowed to make. It's beneficial to indicate both actions players can and cannot do, to ensure they fully understand their options. For example, if players can only move to adjacent squares in your game, you may wish to include a diagram indicating the player can move up, down, left, or right, but not to a diagonal space.

Your visuals should also match the game. Icons, pictures, designs, and colours should be consistent throughout, in order to avoid any confusion. They should be clear and understandable. Also, if there are common symbols that players are used to such as a flame for fire, it's best to use this rather than coming up with something original that might confuse players.

WALK THROUGH THE PROPER STEPS IN ORDER

To help players learn your game for the first time, I suggest including the following sections in your rules in this order:

1. What your game is about and the roles of all players (intro and theme)

2. How to win (goal/objective)

3. Set up (including pictures of the layout to get players started)

4. How to play (including examples and visuals)

5. Things to keep in mind during the game

6. Exceptions ("weird" scenarios and clarifications)

7. Scoring and endgame

8. Notes for easy reference (a reminder section for players to refer to for key points)

9. A legend, including icons, terminology, and anything else of importance

You may also wish to include reference cards or sheets. These are supplements that players can keep in front of them in order to refer back to important rules and actions they can take on their turn. These often include text and visuals to help players remember the steps in your game. Good examples include the reference cards used in *Pandemic* and *Forbidden Island*.

Reference cards are a great way for players to learn your game and can act as a rule summary. Also, if every player has one of these in front of them, they won't need to share and pass around a rulebook. I've often created and tweaked reference cards, which I have later used to help in putting together the rulebook.

To help players refresh their memory or refer back to actions they can take in a game, you may also want to consider the following:

- Icons

- FAQs

- Include the sequence of steps or actions on the game board if one is used (example: *Pandemic*, once again)

Share your rules with players who have played your game as well as those who have not. Let them walk through your rules and ensure that they understand them.

Now it's time to run your first unguided playtest! What's that you ask? You're about to find out...

ACTION: Set up your rules using the order outlined in this chapter. Strongly consider creating player reference cards as well if this will benefit the players. Ensure that your rules work well both for new players to your game, as well as a reference point for all players. Look over your rules to ensure all steps are in place, consistent terminology and visuals are used throughout, and that it is easy to find crucial information. Have at least one other person look over your rules before unguided playtesting and give you honest feedback.

CHAPTER 20
UNGUIDED PLAYTESTING

"Too many games are made for the challenge of it, without seeming to care that much about players. Even though players are important, their reactions should only be taken as feedback you can use to make better games. Player comments shouldn't feed your ego or damage your self-esteem."

- Duane Alan Hahn, video game developer

So, you may be asking yourself "what is unguided (or blind) playtesting?" Unguided is probably a better and more accurate term for this, so we'll use this terminology.

This is the next step in your playtesting journey, and it's called unguided playtesting because it involves people playing your game either without your presence, or with you there, but without you helping in any way. Your involvement will be limited to observing, taking notes, and understanding what challenges players may have when you're not around to help. The gold standard would involve others observing an unguided playtest for you and taking detailed notes, however this is not always feasible due to cost and availability.

Let's dive a little deeper into unguided playtesting now.

HOW TO KNOW YOU'RE READY FOR UNGUIDED PLAYTESTING

Once you've run a number of playtests, fixed any issues, and continued to improve your game, you should find that it runs fairly smoothly. The game should provide a consistent experience across playtests, one that is in line with your expectations, keeps players engaged, and provides a great experience.

There should be very few, if any, "if, then" exceptions in your game. You don't want to have players looking at the rules every five minutes to try to figure things out every time something different happens. Once you reach the point where you are receiving very little feedback, and any suggestions you get are mostly just "different" ideas rather than improvements, you are likely ready for unguided playtesting.

There is no magic number of playtests you have to go through before you're ready for unguided playtesting, as this will differ considerably with each and every game. However, when you have met the criteria above, and players are asking not only to play again, but also when and where they can buy your game, this is a sign that you're on the right track!

Some designers like to jump into unguided playtesting much earlier in the process, which does have some advantages. This will really give you a feel for how your rules work and if there is a more intuitive way for players to play your game. But the downsides are that it is more difficult to get others to commit to learning your game on their own over you teaching them and people can only play your game unguided once. So, you won't be able to run an unguided playtest with them in the later stages of development.

HOW TO RUN AN UNGUIDED PLAYTEST

In most cases, an unguided playtest will basically involve you handing over your game box to a group of playtesters, including the rules and all the components, and letting them figure out how both set up and play the game by themselves. As tempting as it may be, you don't want to interject or answer any questions. This can be really hard, as you'll want to do this automatically, but you'll have to fight the urge. Let them make mistakes and misinterpret the rules. It's better to catch these now as opposed to once the game has already been published.

Your job is to observe. Watch how players play your game, note the reactions they have at different points, and watch their body language along with how engaged they are in the game. You're going to want to take a lot of notes, and once again make improvements and clarify anything that wasn't followed as you would have expected.

There are a number of possible issues you may uncover at this point. For example, players could misinterpret one or more of the rules, they could play something incorrectly, or take actions out of order.

Remember that this is your game and you have to take ownership. If they're not doing something correctly, it's not them playing badly, it's because you didn't communicate this well. Communication, whether in person or through how your rules are written, is so important, not only in gaming, but in life in general.

Go back to your rulebook and update or clarify anything that was confusing. It's through these observations that you'll be able to make improvements to ensure that the next group of playtesters won't run into these same issues.

You might also find that players do something a bit differently than you have outlined. It may be more intuitive for them to do A before B instead of vice-versa. If this makes more sense, don't be afraid to make a change that will ultimately improve your game.

One tactic that some designers use is to film playtesters as they play the game. Just make sure that all playtesters agree to this before you try this method. There are some distinct advantages to this approach. First, you don't have to be present, so the players may react more naturally and won't be worried about hurting your feelings. Secondly, you'll have all gameplay and reactions caught on film, allowing you to watch through and identify where any issues occur. You'll be able to watch these videos again whenever you choose.

It's also possible to hire a service to do unguided playtesting for you. This can be a great option to get some truly unbiased feedback, and especially helpful if you have difficulty finding playtesters or live in a remote area. To make this more helpful to you, make sure that you're using this approach when your game is at a late stage in development, not early on. This option will of course cost you money, so you have to weigh the pros and cons. If it helps to improve your game, then it may be worthwhile.

These types of services are available through companies such as the Indie Game Alliance. You might also want to check out the Tabletop Playtesters Guild Group on Facebook as another option or the list of playtesting groups available on Cardboard Edison.

MAKE SURE YOU HAVE A SOLID RULEBOOK

When you get to the point that you're ready to start unguided playtesting, your rules must be really tight. All scenarios and anomalies should have been uncovered by now as best as possible. This was covered in detail in the previous chapter, but it's worth discussing a bit further.

Remember that you won't be there when someone buys your game and plays it for the first time. Players must be able to run through the game without you being there.

It's also useful to have someone else read over your rules before you start unguided playtesting in order to ensure they make sense. It may help to have both someone who is familiar with your game, as well as someone who has never played it, review your rules to ensure they are understandable.

In the next section, we're going to look at ways to take your game from good to great and from great to amazing.

ACTION: Run your first unguided playtest by handing over your game and letting the players figure it out by themselves. Observe and take notes on how they interpret the rules and gameplay, capturing anywhere the rules weren't followed the way you expected or were confusing to the players. Make sure not to interrupt or interfere. Just observe and take notes. Continue to use the **4 I's Framework** and run further unguided playtests, improving your game with every new version.

SECTION 5

HOW TO TURN A GOOD GAME INTO AN AMAZING GAME

CHAPTER 21
HOW TO CREATE AN INNOVATIVE BOARD GAME (AND WHY THIS IS SO IMPORTANT)

"I think it's wrong that only one company makes the game Monopoly."

- Steven Wright, Comedian

It's very easy to create a game that feels like some other game. But if you're only making one little change or just re-theming it, why would anyone choose to play (or buy) your game rather than that other super popular one they already know and probably already own?

At the same time, if you create something so off-the-wall that people can't really understand it or it just feels way too different, you can alienate potential fans as well.

Rather, you need to look at innovation.

Meriam-Webster (merriam-webster.com) defines innovation as 1. a new idea, device, or method; 2. the act or process of introducing new ideas, devices, or methods.

Innovation is different from invention, which by definition is creating something entirely new. Innovation is really about using new ideas to change an existing thing – in this case, a board game.

WHY INNOVATION IS THE WAY TO GO

People like familiarity. But they also like to see things that are new and different. This is where innovation comes in.

Replication will have people asking why they should buy this rather than an existing game, whereas a wacky new invention may be too different or strange for many people to fully get behind.

If you can create a game that has elements that are familiar and add in some new and innovative twists, you'll greatly increase the chances that players and publishers alike will really take to this.

Century Spice Road is an engine-building game that I have heard referred to as the "*Splendor* killer", as it incorporates some similar mechanics to the elegant gem collecting game but adds some interesting twists. Both games are fantastic in my mind but *Century Spice Road* may have never come to be if it weren't for *Splendor* being introduced first, much like *Dominion* had to come first before other deck-builders could follow.

It's important to understand and appreciate that innovation takes place in stages. A new mechanic or different way of playing may be introduced, then other games will come along, use that mechanic or system, and do something new and innovative with it. But if that drastically different game came first, it very likely would have flopped because it was too far ahead of its time.

The truth is that coming up with an all-new mechanic is hard. Very few completely new mechanics are introduced to the gaming world over time, as so many have already been done before.

It's like music in some ways. There are lots of different chords you can play, but just try to come up with a new one that no one has heard before.

Yet, music has been around forever and probably always will be. Musicians will just play those chords in different patterns and experiment to make their songs and their sound different, sometimes combining different genres, or adding new elements, sounds, and samples.

Rather than trying to create a completely new mechanic, you're in a better position to combine mechanics in a new way or introduce unused or underused themes to make your game stand out.

HOW TO CREATE AN INNOVATIVE BOARD GAME

There are many ways you can incorporate innovation into your game. I'll walk through some methods and include examples as well.

If you can take something familiar, say deck building or card drafting, and add some kind of innovative twist to it, you could have people saying, "Wow, that's really cool!"

Seven Wonders and *Sushi Go* both use a pick-and-pass drafting mechanic that feels quite different from many other games. This allows people the choice of picking something they want or denying other players what they are collecting (commonly referred to as "hate drafting"). But it also adds an element of surprise, as you don't know what will be passed to you or which cards in your hand that you've just passed will come back around to you.

Or you could find a way to combine existing mechanics from different games in a way that's never been done before.

Clank!, for example, builds on the deck-building mechanism by adding a board that allows you to make point-to-point movements and collect treasures from different paths. While deck-building is often the main mechanic in a game (*Dominion, Star Realms*), it is not completely at the forefront in *Clank!*, rather just one part of the game.

Isle of Cats, which is one of my favourites, incorporates a pick-and-pass style draft with an innovative twist: You pick multiple cards most of the rounds rather than just one but you have to pay for whichever of the 7 cards in your hand at the end of the round you'd like to keep. If you don't want them or can't afford them, you have to discard these. But *Isle of Cats* also combines this with drafting of the polyomino cats you must rescue, along with a spatial puzzle for placing your cats on your boat. Your placements dictate which rewards and points you will score, both immediately and at the end of the game.

You could even look at an innovative theme that hasn't been done before or at least not in the way that your game has incorporated this theme.

An obvious example that comes to mind is *Wingspan*. There have been many other engine-building games before this one, but the theme of birds, along with the beautiful artwork and approachable gameplay has led to this becoming an incredibly successful game.

Another example I want to share is *Exploding Kittens*. Whether this game is your cup of tea or not, you can't argue with its success. It was one of the highest funding Kickstarter games ever and continues to sell like bonkers. What they did was essentially take the game of *Russian Roulette* and turned it into a (much safer to play) card game. Combining this with the art of the famous internet comic creator The Oatmeal, it became a hit.

The publisher, who is also known by the name *Exploding Kittens*, has gone on to create many other innovative games, such as *Throw Throw Burrito*, which basically turns a card game into dodgeball.

Up next, we'll talk about how to marry your theme and mechanics in a way that will greatly enhance the experience of your players.

ACTION: Think about what is innovate about your game. If you're not sure about this, ask players what they like about your game and if there's anything about it they've never seen before or never seen done in the way you've created. This innovation may end up being that hook you'll need to wow a publisher or show potential backers what's so cool and different about your game.

CHAPTER 22
MARRYING THE THEME AND MECHANICS IN YOUR BOARD GAME

"Without theme games are a bundle of arbitrary rules, and with the wrong theme those rules are actively confusing and off-putting."

- James Margaris, Blogger

Here's a question that new game designers ask all the time: Should I start with theme or mechanics? I would argue that it doesn't matter where you start as long as you end up with theme and mechanics that are in strong alignment.

But your game doesn't even need to start with a theme or a game mechanic. I often talk about how I feel that the vision for the game is a better starting point. The vision will really outline what experience you are creating for your players and will help guide you in the right direction as you get feedback and make changes to make your game better.

To help you identify the vision for your game and get you moving ahead faster, make sure to check out my 10 Minute Board Game Design Blueprint (bit.ly/bgblueprint).

However, I've had ideas for games that have come from many different sources - theme, mechanic, vision, or even a name that popped into my head.

The starting point isn't nearly as important as the end point.

While working on an early version of your game, you won't know exactly what theme and mechanics will stay and which ones just won't function well. You're simply testing out ideas to see what works and what doesn't.

But over time, you'll want to ensure that the theme and mechanics really align well in your game.

So, let's take a closer look at how to marry your theme and mechanics well to provide a more immersive board game experience for your players.

DO ALL NAMES NEED A STRONG THEME?

First, we should look at the question of whether a board game really needs a theme or not.

There are plenty of examples of great abstract games with little or no real theme. For example, *Chess*, *Go*, *Tak*, and *Blokus*.

There are also lots of fantastic games where the theme is pretty light and could be interchangeable with just about any theme. Consider for example, *Azul*, *Sagrada*, or *Santorini*.

So, we can see that a game can be both successful and well-designed without necessarily having a theme.

At the same time, a theme can draw you into a game and make it a much more immersive experience. But sometimes forcing a theme onto your game will lead players to say that the theme is "pasted on." In other words, the theme it's pretty interchangeable - it's not an integral part of the game at all.

It's usually a good idea to have some kind of a theme on your game rather than go for a very black and white abstract feel like *Chess* or *Go*. If you end up pitching your game to publishers and it gets signed, they will be the ones to ultimately decide on the theme, but having some sort of theme will make your game more accessible and will likely generate more interest from a publisher.

So, the answer is no, every game doesn't necessarily need a theme, however, it's more likely to be successful if there is some sort of theme associated with the game. So, if you can figure out a theme that works well for your game, go for it!

MARRYING THEME AND MECHANICS IN YOUR GAME

A rich theme can really draw people into your game. It can make players feel that they are part of this specific world that you've created.

In order to truly integrate your theme and mechanics, you'll want to think about what roles the players are playing as and understand the world that they live in and what they would want to try to accomplish, and how they would go about doing this.

I've co-designed a game called *License to Grill*, which is about trying to outdo your friends at a barbecue by taking over the grill and cooking your orders to perfection. In real life, when you want to cook a meal well, you have to pay attention to things like the temperature and cooking time. Not only that, you may want to marinate your food or baste it with some sauce while it's cooking.

So, we made sure that the focus would be on time and resource management. Everyone has a limited number of actions they can take on their turn, which would mimic what you might be able to accomplish in a couple minutes in real life. You can't do everything at once, so you'll have to decide whether to focus your time on putting a new order on the grill, taking something off, or serving your food.

However, you're sharing the grill with all the other players, and some may decide to turn up the heat, so you'll have to react and try to get your orders off the grill at the best possible time.

All the actions and gameplay are very thematic, because they are the types of things you would think about if you were really sharing a grill with your friends and trying to outdo them in real life.

You just have to be careful that your game doesn't turn into a simulation, which is a different experience entirely. You're making a game, so it should still be fun and engaging, not just replicating real life tasks.

You'll want to think about what types of resources players would want to get and how they would obtain them. Are there berries that will ripen somewhat randomly at different times? Will players have to race to get what they need? Would it make more sense for players to buy these things at an auction?

Also, think about the mechanics that would best fit into this experience.

Is there a lot of risk-taking in your game that would fit well with a press your luck mechanic? Are you sending off workers to complete tasks, in which a worker placement mechanic might work best? Are players collecting items that would become more valuable the more they have? Set collection may work perfectly in this situation.

CLOSING THOUGHTS ON THEME AND MECHANICS

In order to marry theme and mechanics well in your game, you really want to think about what's happening in your game and the roles that players will take on. Determine how they would need to accomplish their goals and what makes sense for them to get there.

Also, make sure to ask players how they feel about the theme. Does it match with what they're doing? Are there other actions they would like to take but can't?

Over time, you may realize that your theme just isn't working or maybe that your mechanics are not aligned with your theme. It's OK to change either of these. Or both! When you're designing a game, nothing is set in stone. Any changes that make your game better while still holding to the vision you have for your game are always worth considering.

Next up, we'll go into how and why you need to simplify your game.

ACTION: When you're working on your game, continue to ask yourself if the theme and mechanics match well. Listen to feedback and make any necessary changes to make your game more thematic and in line with player expectations.

CHAPTER 23

WHY YOU NEED TO SIMPLIFY YOUR GAME

"Simplify, simplify."

- Henry David Thoreau, Philosopher

Let's face it. You just worked a long day. Maybe you had to go through negotiation, bribery, and warfare to get your kids to bed. You're finally caught up on all the chores on your to-do list. Now you just want to settle down into a nice game with your partner or a few friends.

The last thing you want to do is spend the next hour poring over a complex rulebook trying to understand how to play the game you just shelled out 60 bucks for. You'd rather ease right into a game and experience the world outside of your normal reality.

So, instead of trying out that new game you've had sitting on your shelf of shame (or shelf of opportunity, depending on your perspective) that you've been eager to play, you just grab whatever game off your shelf is familiar.

Does this sound like you? Well, this is a common feeling among many gamers.

When designing a game, it's important to remember what it's like the first time we open a new game and try to figure out how it's played.

KEEP THIS IN MIND TO GET MORE PEOPLE TO PLAY YOUR GAME

We have to remember that most people are casual gamers, not hard-core hobbyists who don't mind spending a lot of time trying to figure out a game.

We have to remember that simplicity is elegance.

That's not to say that your game should be as simple and uninteresting as *Tic-Tac-Toe*. But it should be easy to grasp right away. The true experience for players is then in the tricky choices and gameplay that will keep them coming back for more.

Take *Azul* for example.

The concept is simple. Take all the tiles of one colour from one of the factory displays of your choice, slide the rest of the tiles into the center, and place your chosen tile(s) on your board. What could be easier?

The challenge comes in deciding which tile you should choose based on what would benefit you and/or what will make things more difficult for your opponent(s), along with where you will place tiles in order to maximize your score, balancing between short-term and long-term goals.

Compare this to a game where players have to make a choice between 10 different options, keep track of multiple things, remember to take specific actions at the end of their turn, and pass something to the next player. Now every player must complete the same steps, which ends phase 1. Did I mention there are six phases before the first round is over?

Why take a chance on something so complex?

That's not to say that there isn't a market for complex games with a huge number of decision points, many different phases, and an extensive rulebook, but this type of game will likely appeal less to most casual gamers, who make up the majority of the market.

WHAT TO WATCH FOR WHEN PLAYTESTING YOUR GAME

When you're playtesting your game and you notice that people stop paying attention as you're reading or explaining the rules, have to constantly ask questions throughout the game, or there is a lot of confusion about gameplay and player actions, then your game might be too complex.

The answer is to simplify. This doesn't mean you should make your game simplistic, rather make it easier to understand, and with perhaps less actions or choices at different points.

Try reducing it down by removing one aspect or decreasing the number of things a player does on their turn. I have found that giving players a choice of 3-5 different options that are all potentially beneficial in some way is a good range to aim for. Sometimes you can get away with more than this, but this range seems to work well in most cases.

When it comes to resources, I've heard strong arguments to keep them to 5-6 or less. Much more than this makes it difficult for players to keep track of everything and may slow down your game or make it less fun.

Sometimes even a choice between two interesting and viable options can work really well. The solo game *Friday* is a great example of giving the player a choice between two obstacles to overcome, each giving a different reward, and making for interesting choices and strategies that a player can take.

Many press your luck games, including *Quacks of Quedlinburg*, *Port Royal*, *Incan Gold*, and *Can't Stop* give you two simple choices each turn – stop or continue. Do you risk it to get more points or gold, with the possibility of losing it all, or stop and collect what you've already gained? This can make for some highly memorable moments when a player either pulls off a miracle comeback or goes down in flames, losing a huge gain.

The more choices a player has, the more likely they will fall into AP (analysis paralysis). The longer one player takes to make a decision, the longer other players will have to wait for their turn, which is something you want to avoid. Quick or simultaneous turns, or at least something for players to strategize while it is not their turn, is something to strive for and something that will often lead to more player engagement.

By making some changes and simplifying your game, you might just increase engagement and improve the overall flow. If players have less time between their turns, but still have enough to think about and plan for in between, then you're probably on the right track.

Another element that can make for a better experience is surprise, which is what the next chapter is all about.

ACTION: Take a closer look at your game. Explore every turn, round, and phase. Are there any steps or rules that are complicated or get in the way of the fun? Are there any actions that you can remove that may make the game better and flow more smoothly?

Don't be afraid to remove or alter some aspect of your game and playtest this change to see if it improved your game. You might be surprised to discover that something you thought was crucial wasn't actually needed at all!

CHAPTER 24

HOW TO SURPRISE YOUR PLAYERS (AND WHY YOU WANT TO DO THIS)

"Games were not just a diversion, I realized. Games could make you feel."

- Sid Meier, Game Designer

When you're designing a game, you'll want to come up with something new and innovative. Something players haven't seen done before. If you can find a way to surprise your players, you'll increase the interest, curiosity, and replay value of your game.

If you can find a way to make your players say, "Wow, that's so cool!" then you know you've hit on something special.

There are many ways to implement the element of surprise in your game, so in this chapter we'll delve into a number of these reasons along with why it's a good idea to find ways to surprise your players.

WHY YOU WANT TO SURPRISE YOUR PLAYERS

There are definitely some great benefits to creating familiarity in your game. Most players are familiar with tiling, set collection, worker placement, deck building, and various other mechanics in board games. Recognizing something that you already know makes it much easier to get into the game and understand it faster. Understanding a game faster means there's more chance your game will get played.

But at the same time, your game can't just be a re-skin of another popular game. Otherwise, why wouldn't players just play that other game that they're already familiar with and probably already own?

That's where innovation comes in. Blending something familiar with another aspect that is innovative and new is a great approach to designing a game and increasing its chance of success.

You want players to react to your game with joy, enthusiasm, and if possible, amazement.

If players feel there will always be something new and interesting they will discover in your game or another strategy they can try, this will keep players coming back for more, showing this game to their friends, and having more people discover your game. It will add to the replay value of your game so that not only more people will buy your game, but they will also play it a whole lot more.

I call that a win-win.

GIVE PLAYERS SOMETHING TO LOOK FORWARD TO

There are plenty of ways to make players want to come back to your game again and again.

One of those ways is to create multiple paths to victory. If you allow (and hopefully also encourage) players to take various strategies, each having some chance of success, it will allow players to more fully explore your game and try different things every time they play.

If you have a large deck of cards and only a small number of them will be revealed each game, it allows for a feeling of surprise when a new card is drawn and/or played, especially if it is something that players haven't seen done before. Every card in the deck doesn't need to be like this, but the role of discovery in finding these few really cool cards can make for some magic moments in your game. If there are still plenty of cards that haven't been seen yet, this gives players more curiosity, as they want to see what's coming next.

If your game is more of a campaign-style or legacy game, there are plenty of ways to introduce new parts of the story, new components, new mechanics, and variations in gameplay as players move from one stage of the game to the next. You don't want to overwhelm players by giving them too many new things to learn, so introducing one cool new thing every time they advance to a certain level can be a fun experience for players.

EVERYBODY LOVES A GOOD COMBO

Maybe you've created cards or powers in your game that synergize really well. Players won't know this going into the game, but as they play it more and draw different combinations every time they play, they may discover some cool combos they can pull off.

Everybody loves a good combo. Whether it's a fighting game, engine building game, or other style of game, you feel really smart when you put two and two together and somehow make five. It feels great when you discover that combining different cards or effects will make you that much more powerful. Finding ways to make players feel clever is always a positive step for your game.

SURPRISE YOUR PLAYERS IN OTHER WAYS

Have you ever opened up a board game box and been delightfully surprised by the quality of the components, a nice concise rule book, or a beautiful layout with just the right insert?

You can and absolutely should try to surprise your players with something amazing related to the gameplay but you can also include interesting and high-quality components there will also surprise and delight players.

If you self-published your game through crowdfunding, you may even want to include a surprise extra component or promo card or even some sort of personalized message to your backer.

Think about what would surprise and delight you when you open your game. Then aim to include something of this nature in your game.

Remember back to the days of opening a new game you were really excited about and discovering something that made it an even better experience. This may have been related to the components, something extra, or the gameplay itself. Use these ideas and lessons and incorporate something similar into your game.

In addition to surprise, creating magical moments that happen in your game can also be quite appealing to players. We'll go into this next in just a moment.

ACTION: What game surprised and delighted you? What did this game do differently than others to get your attention? Give this some thought and then think about what you could do with your own game to surprise and delight new players.

CHAPTER 25
CREATING MEMORABLE MOMENTS IN YOUR GAME

"Games can have incredible moments where something sears itself into memory, when a story is born for you to tell time and again."

- Zach Barash, Game Designer

Memorable moments are something you really want to aim for when you're designing your game. They bring more excitement and can help a publisher see why they would want to sign and publish your game, or in the case of self-publishing, help your audience to understand why they would enjoy your game so much.

There are so many ways to create memorable moments in a game, so I'll just touch on some of the many helpful examples here, along with the game mechanics that really help bring them to life.

CREATING MEMORABLE MOMENTS THROUGH LAUGHTER

People will often remember something funny that they heard or that happened to them. That's why party games can often create these memorable moments.

Telestrations is a great example. It's essentially "broken telephone" with drawings. Unlike some drawing games, the worse of an artist you are, the funnier and better the game becomes.

"Remember that time I drew a dog and you thought it was an alligator getting high?" Now that's a memorable moment!

My family used to play *Balderdash* every Christmas at my grandma's house. We always had a great time and a lot of laughs. Years later we still laugh about the time when my cousin defined "Scotophobia" as the fear of my grandpa (whose last name was Scott) taking off his shirt. He had actually done this earlier in the afternoon when he was feeling too hot, so hearing someone come out and say this was hilarious!

Or the time that my uncle simply wrote down the definition of some random word as "A buzzard's udder." Pretty soon everyone around the table was getting in on the gag and each round after that featured at least one answer involving a buzzard's udder. This became a regular inside joke for us.

Those are a few memorable moments that I will always cherish.

Allowing players to use their creativity will end up with unpredictable results, which have the potential to be remembered for many years to come.

CREATING MEMORABLE MOMENTS THROUGH UNBELIEVABLE PLAYS

Games that allow you to push your luck can often create memorable moments as well.

I recall playing an online prototype of a push your luck pirate game created by my friend AJ Brandon. Every space you sailed would either lead you to treasures or more danger. If you go too far you'll lose it all to your opponent.

I fell way behind in the first round, but then in the second round, I somehow timed my 2 cannonballs at the exact right time to take out the other pirate ships and gain a whopping load of treasure to take a big lead.

This was definitely a memorable moment that we'll all recall and laugh over later.

I've mentioned other push your luck games like *Incan Gold* and *Can't Stop* previously. These types of games allow players to make incredible comebacks if they're willing to take the risk.

These unbelievable plays can also be achieved through engine building and chaining together different combinations.

Even something as simple as a roll-and-write game can accomplish this. Take *Ganz Schon Clever* (*That's Pretty Clever*) for example.

When you check off certain boxes, this will trigger earning additional rewards which can be placed elsewhere on your board, which when placed at the right time will trigger even more rewards. This is an example of chaining.

Even including the simple luck of the roll in a game like *Dungeons and Dragons (D&D)* can allow for some big swings and memorable moments.

People will remember what happened within the context of the game. They won't say "Remember that time you rolled two 20s in a row?" Instead, they'll recall that moment and say, "Remember when you finished off that dragon with your broken spear when he was just about to scorch our whole party?"

There are so many ways to create memorable moments in your game. As you're working on your own game design, watch for those moments when something big and memorable happens. Double down on this. Find ways to bring out these memorable moments even more often.

But it's not always easy to direct your players towards those memorable moments. Sometimes you need to provide incentives for them to do a certain action or take a risk. That's what our next chapter is all about.

ACTION: Think about what the most memorable moment you've experienced in a game. Why was it so memorable? Keep this in mind as you're designing your game and watch for these memorable moments when you're playtesting. Once you discover where these memorable moments lie in your game, see if you can find ways to bring them out more often and create an even better experience for your players.

CHAPTER 26
INCENTIVIZING PLAYERS AND PROVIDING THEM WITH SOME DIRECTION

"A game is a series of interesting choices."

– Sid Meier, Game Designer

Quite often when you're designing a game you find that players don't do the types of things you want them to. Instead of collecting and trading resources, one player might be amassing a fortune in gold, while other players are just exploring the island, for example.

So, how do we as game designers ensure that players are taking the actions that we intended for them and guide them towards their ultimate goal?

USING GAME MECHANICS FOR INCENTIVIZING PLAYERS TO DO WHAT YOU WANT

In order for players to take on certain strategies, go after particular items, or travel in a specific direction, you have to give them a reason to do so.

This can be accomplished in one of many ways. Often, it comes down to rewards and punishment. You want to reward players for going down the correct path and/or give consequences when they don't.

It's all part of a feedback loop. The right actions lead to good things, and the wrong actions put you further behind.

Let's look at some examples of games that do this well.

Splendor is a great example because it's such a simple and elegant game that does things so well.

The intention in *Splendor* is for you as the player to collect enough gem tokens to start buying cards and then chain them together to buy better cards and start collecting more valuable cards with point values, as well as the Noble tiles.

If you simply continue to collect tokens, it will be very hard, if not impossible, to gather enough to purchase point cards. At the same time, if you only collect cards from the first row that don't contain any points, you may end up with a lot of cards but it will be hard to win, as you need to gain 15 points to achieve victory. You'll watch as other players trade up their tokens and use their cards, leaving you in the dust.

Splendor also makes it very clear that your goal is to get 15 points and shows you how to get there.

Barenpark is another good example. It makes use of polyomino (*Tetris*-like) tiles that you must place in your park. Whenever you cover a symbol with your piece, you will gain the associated structure or an additional park expansion board.

When you complete each of the 4 boards in your park, you will get to place a bear pit. The first bear pit is worth the most points and each one after this is worth a little less, so you're incentivized to complete each of your 4 boards quickly to gain more points. However, you must figure out exactly how you'll go about doing this through the pieces (structures) you gather and where you place them.

As you can see from these examples, including game mechanics where players gain something from taking actions you would like them to do, makes for strong incentives.

GIVE YOUR PLAYERS A CLEAR DIRECTION

While you want to give your players interesting choices to make throughout your game, you also want to ensure that these choices matter and the players can make a well-informed decision.

If you start them off blindly in a game with no direction at all, many players will struggle right out of the gate. They won't even know what to do on their first turn.

I often see this in other prototypes (and sometimes in my own!). Players are given a wealth of options but no clear direction. They may know that they have to have the most points at the end of the game to win but may not have any clue what a good move looks like to earn those points.

There are a few things you can do to help players.

One way to accomplish this is through hidden objective cards. A good example of this is from the game *Sanssouci* by Michael Keisling (the designer of *Azul*).

In *Sanssouci*, you are given 2 goal cards that indicate you will get bonus points at the end of the game for moving pawns down specific paths. Without this direction and additional incentive, players may have difficulty drafting tiles, as they all might otherwise feel like each tile will provide fairly similar outcomes.

Many other games, from *Ticket to Ride* to *Lords of Waterdeep* use hidden objective cards as well.

You can also provide your players with direction by using public objectives or goals that any player can accomplish. You can even incentivize them further by having reduced rewards over time, as we see with the bear pits in *Barenpark*.

Otherwise, just make it obvious to players what they need to achieve and the possible ways they can accomplish this.

If your game is about fighting monsters, make the core loop of your game clear to players. For example, if you fight a monster you earn gold. You then spend your gold on better weapons to make yourself more powerful and be able to fight bigger and badder monsters (gaining bigger rewards).

By making the end goal, along with how to accomplish this, very clear, and possibly giving players specific things to accomplish along the way, you'll be incentivizing them to do what you wish and pointing them in the right direction right from the start.

In the next chapter, we'll discuss how to keep your players engaged throughout your game.

ACTION: Consider the things you want players to do most in your now. Now look at whether they are incentivized to take these actions. You want players to feel a sense of reward or accomplishment, so make sure to build this feedback into your game and incentive structure.

Also, if players are feeling overwhelmed with options at the start of your game or have no idea what to do first, look at ways to provide them with some direction. This may be through private goal cards, player powers, or a path that looks to have value or a limited resource that they'll want to grab before everyone else.

CHAPTER 27
HOW TO KEEP PLAYERS ENGAGED

"In the last ~15 years, tabletop games seem to have become less competitive/cutthroat overall. I theorize it's because video games are so much better at competitive environments, that's where competitive players go now. The remaining demand for tabletop games is thus more social."

- Nick Bentley, Underdog Games Studio

It's important to keep players engaged throughout your game. But what do we mean when we say we want to keep players engaged?

Well, rather than looking at their phone, staring off into space, or getting easily distracted, we want players to stay focused on the game in front of them and feel compelled to pay attention and enjoy the experience at hand.

So, without further ado let's look at how to keep players engaged in your game.

SHORT, QUICK TURNS OR SIMULTANEOUS PLAY

Incorporating quick turns and simultaneous play are important methods to keep your players playing rather than sitting around waiting for their turn to eventually come around. Those long pauses in between play are an easy way for players to lose engagement.

While it's not always possible in all game types to keep turns quick and snappy, if you can do so it will definitely help keep players engaged and improve the flow of your game.

Rather than allowing a player to do 5 actions on their turn, try just allowing them to do one or two actions and limit their options to a small number of available choices.

A great example of this is *Splendor*. You do one of four things on your turn, then it passes on to the next player. The best decision isn't necessarily obvious, but your options are intuitive and quick choices can be made.

When your players are often saying "Oh it's my turn again?", you know you've got a game that's moving at a good pace.

High engagement can also be achieved by using simultaneous play. Essentially, it boils down to revealing something that is available to everyone and allowing each player to decide exactly how they want to use it on their own board or play area.

One of my favourites in this realm is *Cartographers*.

A terrain type and shape are revealed (cards have either 2 terrain types and 1 shape or 1 terrain type and 2 shapes), and you must figure out where to best place them in order to score points with the given objectives.

The variation in objectives from game to game makes this a different puzzle every time you play.

GAME MECHANICS THAT GIVE PLAYERS SOMETHING TO THINK ABOUT

Another way to keep players engaged is by presenting them with something to do when it's not their turn. This could involve planning, negotiating with other players, or looking at the options available to them and determining the best strategies.

Co-operative games like *Flashpoint: Fire Rescue* often allow players to take multiple actions on their turn, which can make for less-than-quick turns. However, players remain engaged because they are constantly planning with other players to figure out what the best moves are on each player's turn and how they should plan ahead together. They have to figure out what is a high priority and what can wait. You only succeed by working together.

In a think-y game like *Santorini*, where you have to figure out a way to build, move, and get your character to the top of a building first, you're constantly thinking ahead and assessing the board state. You may take a minute or two coming up with the best move, but at the same time, your opponent is trying to figure out your strategy and how to counter or work around it.

It's much like *Chess* in that way. You don't want the game to move too quickly, because you want time to think and make the best move possible. This often works best in a 2-player game, as only one other player is waiting to take their turn, and they have plenty to think about. The board will also not change drastically by the time they get to move again.

Now, if you can incorporate quick turns and something to think about when it's not your turn (as long as it's not too onerous or slows down the game), you've got a great combination going!

Players may feel unengaged however, if the balance of your game is off (or even it they perceive it to be unbalanced). So, we'll tackle this in the next chapter.

ACTION: How do you ensure players are highly engaged in your game? Consider what players are doing when it's their turn but also what they are doing when it's another player's turn. If players have something to do while they are waiting for their turn, such as strategizing, negotiating, or looking and figuring out how to best use the card they just drew, this can keep them engaged. Keeping turns quick or simultaneous can have the same effect. So, watch for any lulls in your game and look for ways to make it more engaging.

CHAPTER 28
BALANCING YOUR GAME

"There is no such thing as perfect balance... There are too many variables that a designer can not control, and should not try to."

- Blood and Spectacles Blog

I'm often asked by other game designers for tips on how to balance a game. It's a tricky thing. You don't normally want your game to be too "swingy" (although in some games this IS exactly what you want) but at the same time, if you make a game that is too linear, it can quickly become boring and predictable.

So, it's good to think about how you can make your game reasonably well-balanced, without any cards, powers, or strategies that are over-powered (OP).

Let's look at some ways that you can balance your game.

TEST DIFFERENT STRATEGIES

I'm a big advocate for self-playtesting. I'll set up players' positions around the table and play as multiple players competing against each other (or working together in the case of a co-op game).

But the trick is to self-playtest with a goal in mind. Usually, that goal for me is testing different strategies. I want to know which strategies are viable and at least stand a chance of winning and which do not.

However, it's really easy to lose track of who is going after what when you're trying to play a game 3 or 4-handed all by yourself. So, I always make sure to write this down on a piece of scrap paper or sticky note and place this in front of each player's spot.

For example, in my flower collection game, *Avoid the Cacti!*, I may write things like "Daffodils", "Roses", "Queen Anne's Lace", and "balanced approach", indicating which flower type each player is aiming for. I will take turns and select flowers for each player based on the type they want, and then I will compare scores and strategies when the game ends.

If one strategy failed miserably but should have been a contender, I will note whether it wasn't viable or if that player just had a bit of bad luck. Then I may change some values and test this again, ensuring that all valid strategies stand a chance at winning, whereas other obviously sub-optimal strategies will not.

This last point is something you definitely want to watch out for. If someone can just collect gold each turn and do nothing else, then claim victory at the end, this is a boring strategy that you probably want to fix to ensure players can tell right away this will not lead them to success.

You can also test your hypotheses while watching others play your game. Note which direction each player takes, notice if they change that strategy part-way through the game, and how close the score was at the end. Understand whether each player actually could have won with each strategy that was taken.

IT'S ALL RELATIVE

When you are balancing costs with their actions or effects, what you really want to do is look at relative values.

Start with a baseline – your least valuable resource or card. Give this a value, say 1, and then scale everything else based on this value. Just make sure not to be too linear in this approach. You want the resources that are harder to get to be much more powerful and worth a player's time to capture them.

For example, if you have a card that costs 1 gold and gives you 2 wheat, you don't want to simply have another card that costs 2 gold and gives you 4 wheat and keep going with this linear line of valuation.

Instead, you may want that card that costs 2 gold to give you 5 wheat. This is more valuable than simply getting two of those cards that cost 1 gold. Perhaps 5 gold will net you 15 wheat. Scale things up to make more costly cards or more challenging objectives worthwhile.

The same goes for set collection. You will notice that many games scale up scoring as you collect more resources of one kind. Often it will be something like 1/3/6/10/15 points for 1/2/3/4/5 of those goods collected. Essentially, the first one will gain you one point, the second will earn you two more points, the third will get you 3 more points, and so on.

PLAYTEST, PLAYTEST, PLAYTEST!

I've said it before and I'll say it again: you need to playtest your game until the point where people are loving your game and asking to play it again or buy it right there on the spot.

You may have spreadsheet upon spreadsheet with all the costs, calculations, and values for each card in your deck, and have figured out the perfect relationship. But if players repeatedly call a certain card weak and never want to purchase it or they feel that one card is OP, you have to listen to what they are saying. If anyone feels that the first player to get a specific card will automatically win, that's a problem.

Even though in reality everything might be very well balanced, if players don't *perceive* your game to be well balanced, this can be problematic. They are not in the know and aware of all your work behind the scenes. They only know what they feel. And if they feel things are out of balance in your game, especially if multiple people are telling you this, you need to listen. This may result in some minor changes that make players feel that everything is fair.

Playtesting with others is the best (and only) way to find out how players really feel about your game and their chances of accomplishing what they set out to do, given the strategy they chose.

So, listen to your playtesters. Don't try to convince them that you've done the math and you're right. Instead, listen to their perceptions and take them into account.

Having a game that is 100% balanced may take the fun right out of it. Instead, aim for a game that feels relatively balanced to yourself and players, where multiple viable strategies and powers all have a fair chance of winning.

In the next chapter, we'll discuss something that many designers, especially new ones, don't often think about when creating their game (but really should!).

ACTION: Hone the balance in your game through testing these strategies thoroughly, determining a solid base value and other values relative to this, and playtesting the heck out of your game. Remember that your game doesn't need to be 100% fully balanced (it's actually often better not to be) but it needs to "feel" like it is balanced to your players. Perception is reality in this case.

CHAPTER 29
3 THINGS YOU CAN DO TO MAKE YOUR GAME A BETTER PRODUCT

"I'm not arguing companies should refrain from publishing new games. I'm arguing they should kill games that aren't among their most promising."

- Nick Bentley, Underdog Games Studio

In this chapter, we're going to look at the top 3 things you can do to make your game a better product. This isn't something that a lot of game designers think about when they are designing a game (especially their first), but it is worth consideration.

After all, publishers may love a game, but at the end of the day they are running a business. You can't run a business without making money. And a board game publisher won't make money unless they put out games that people want to buy.

That's where the idea of looking at your game as a product can be super helpful.

A really fun game is great to play but won't necessarily be found by everyone who might enjoy it if the game isn't marketable (I've definitely been in this situation before).

At the same time, a game that is "gimmicky" and gets people's attention may sell some copies initially, but if players feel it isn't a great game and word spreads, sales will die off.

But…if a publisher recognizes you have an amazing game AND sees how they can market it to their audience, you've got a winning combination.

It's time to look at how you can make your game a better product while you're designing your game.

#3 CLEAR UP ANY FIDDLY RULES

A great rulebook will allow players and publishers to understand your game easily, improving the chances that your game will get played and maybe even published.

You may notice that you have lots of "edge cases", exceptions, and if/then situations in your rules.

Ask yourself: Are all of these rules necessary? Are these rules there as bandaid solutions to things that have come up in playtesting?

If you've added a rule anytime that something came up outside of typical gameplay, you may now have a hodgepodge of rules with a lot of conditions and clauses that are unintuitive or difficult to interpret. It's always a good idea to review and revise your rules, especially following blind playtesting, which is also critical in making your game better.

Rules may not sound like something crucial to making your game a better product at first, but when you think about it, this is the way people will initially learn how to play your game. If they can't figure the rules out, they won't be playing it. Poor instructions can lead people to thinking much less of a product.

#2 PERCEIVED VALUE

When someone is looking at your game in the store, picks it up off the shelf, and checks the price, are they going to turn it over and read the back to learn more about it, or put it back and let it continue to gather dust?

Burgle Bros is a great co-op game, where you work together as thieves to pull off a heist. It has a fairly small, compact box, where everything fits nice and tightly. But when you pull it off the shelf and see the price tag of $63.95 (the price at my local game store), you may stop and think twice. Again, it's a great game, but people may perceive this as overpriced for what you get. This is just one example to get you thinking about perceived value.

Generally, a game will be sold in retail stores for about 5-6 times the landed cost of the game (cost of manufacturing + freight shipping to the destination). That may seem like a lot, but it is marked up by the distributor and retail store, which are both taking on risk when they order copies of a game. If the game sells, they make a nice profit, but if it doesn't they may have to mark it down to cost or even take a loss.

So, putting on your developer hat, it's good to look at ways you can reduce or re-use components. For example, make money and other resources in multiple denominations, not just single values. Look at ways to use cards multiple ways (tops, bottoms, both sides, etc.). See if you can reduce the number of cards, while ensuring the gameplay doesn't suffer (you may find it actually improves your game – I have on multiple games!).

If you can create a game that packs a punch in terms of content, gameplay, and fun, without hurting the wallet, you've got a good product.

#1 THE HOOK

Having a "hook" or a unique selling proposition (USP) for your game is crucial in the current age of board games. Thousands of new titles are being released each year, so if you don't have anything that sets your game apart, you're going to have trouble marketing your game.

I often hear new designers say they don't know what the hook is for their game. If this is one of your first games and you don't intend to publish it, that's ok, but if you're trying to pitch your games to a publisher or get people excited about your upcoming Kickstarter campaign, this is certainly a red flag.

You need to figure out what makes your game both unique and appealing to players. If you're not sure what this is yourself, listen to your playtesters. What are they saying about your game? What do they enjoy most about it? What has them coming back for more?

Think about why your game is innovative. Can your game be played without a table? Does it combine mechanics in a way never seen before? Does it have amazing table presence? Why?

Ask yourself why your game is different and what gets people excited about it. Then home in on this. If you can't figure out your hook, keep working on your game and ensure that you develop a strong hook to get people excited about your game.

This can also help you a lot with your pitch.

Additional Thoughts

If you're working on your first game, I would encourage you to focus on completing it and getting your first game under your belt. Just completing creating a game is an accomplishment in itself. Recognize that your first game probably won't be as good as your fifth game and your fifth game probably won't be as good as your tenth game. Like with most endeavors, you'll improve over time.

But if that first game turns out to be good after all and you decide to get it published, you'll definitely want to be thinking of your game and how to market it as a product.

The more you work on games, the more you'll want to look at how to make them better products. This will make them more publishable, whether you intend to pitch your game to publishers or self-publish your game.

It's important as well to consider how your game should end and how to determine the winner, as there are plenty of different methods you can use. We'll dive deep into these topics in the next chapter.

ACTION: Take off your designer's hat for a moment and look at your game from the perspective of a publisher and a customer. Ask yourself some questions. What makes your game stand out from all the others? Why would someone buy your game over others?

Try to determine whether your game is feasible from a production and cost standpoint. Will people buy your game at the MSRP it will need to be priced at?

All of the above are considerations to make your game a great product.

CHAPTER 30
CREATING COMPELLING VICTORY CONDITIONS

"The goal is to win, but it is the goal that is important, not the winning."

- Reiner Knizia, Game Designer

Victory points (VP) are so common in modern board games, along with the condition that the player at the end of the game with the most VP is declared the winner. Sometimes it is called influence, sometimes just points, or it may be money or some other resource or currency. But it is all essentially the same thing. So, we're going to dive into some other fun and interesting ways that players can win a game, along with examples of each.

However, no discussion of victory conditions would be complete without also talking about end game conditions, as these often go hand-in-hand. Quite often this end game condition will determine the winner, while other times it signals that the game is over or that players have some number of turns left, whether this is for all players, all players other than the player who triggered the end of the game, or all players who hadn't played yet this round (to ensure all players get an equal number of turns).

I will touch on how some of these victory conditions relate to the end game conditions here as well.

So, let's look at some alternatives to victory points.

FIRST TO THE FINISH

A first to the finish win condition is often used in racing games or games meant to feel like a race. Often, the game will end as soon as one player crosses the finish line (or this will at least trigger the end game condition).

An example of this is *Steam Punk Rally*. Well, sort of. You see, once a player crosses the finish line, the last round is triggered, but another player may actually travel farther past the player who crossed the finish line to win the game.

Although I haven't played it myself, *Flamme Rouge* is another example of a game where you have to be first to cross the finish line to claim victory. Many other racing games are quite similar in this regard.

FIRST TO X NUMBER OF POINTS

Another win condition is the first player to amass a certain number of points. This could also be done using money or another resource as well.

A great example of this is *Splendor*. In *Splendor*, when a player gets 15 points, all other players who haven't played yet this round get one more turn. The winner is the player with the most points.

Port Royal and *Century: Spice Road* are very similar in that reaching a certain point value will trigger the end game, allowing any players who hadn't played yet that round one last turn.

Most modern board games try to be fair and allow all players to have the exact same number of turns by the end of the game, as the first player may otherwise have an advantage. So, this is usually used more as an end game condition than a victory condition, as also seen in the examples above.

LAST ONE STANDING (ELIMINATION)

If a game is all about eliminating players, it will often leave one lone player left at the end of the game. This player will be declared the winner.

An excellent example of last one standing is *Coup*. In this game, all players have 2 identity cards. Once both of these cards have been eliminated, you're out. So, the last player left with one or more cards remaining wins.

Another example is a *Texas Hold'em Poker* (usually referrd to as simply "*Hold'em*") tournament. The last player with chips remaining after all other players are eliminated is the winner (usually with a decent cash prize!).

This list would be incomplete without mentioning *Checkers*, in which you win by being the only player with pieces remaining.

FIRST TO ACCOMPLISH A GOAL

Quite often, a game will have an objective or several objectives that players must meet. In some games when a player meets the objective, this simply triggers the end of the game, whereas other times the first to accomplish the goal will be declared the winner.

One example of this is *Machi Koro*. It has many versions, and in the *Bright Lights, Big City* edition that I own, the first to obtain all 6 landmarks is declared the winner.

Many co-op and solo games also take the approach of including an objective that must be reached in order to win the game. In *Pandemic*, you must cure all 4 diseases. In *Flashpoint: Fire Rescue*, you must save 7 people/animals. In *Crystallo*, you must defeat the dragon.

Conversely, many co-op games also have losing conditions (often multiple), such as running out of cards, using up all of one component, or a danger level that has increased too high.

OTHER VICTORY CONDITIONS AND VARIANTS

Quite often, a game will have an end game or victory condition that will be some variation of one of the above or with some other twist.

One that is sometimes common in card games is the first to shed all cards. *Uno*, *President*, and *Zoo Year's Eve* are good examples of this.

Or rather than trying to attain the highest score, some games push you to get the lowest score among all players, such as *Dominos* or the sport of golf. *Blokus* also essentially does this, as you want to have the least remaining pieces.

Ending the game with the majority is a victory condition in some classic games like *Go* and *Othello*.

And of course, there is the famous "capture/eliminate the King (or some other specific piece)" as made famous by *Chess* but also used in other games like *Stratego*. A better, more broad term for this would be "capture the flag", which bears the same name as the outdoor game.

Or you might need to be the first player to make it to a destination (although this might also be considered an objective), as you do in *Chinese Checkers*. Another more modern example of this is the excellent game, *Santorini*, where you have to be the first player to reach the top of a 3-tier building to win.

Another objective is to get a certain number of pieces in a row, as you do in *Tic Tac Toe* and *Connect 4*.

Some social deduction games give you the victory when you're able to identify the spy or another character (or get away with being this character if you are the traitor), as is seen in *The Resistance* and *Spyfall*.

A party game like *Telestrations* doesn't even have scoring! You just play as many rounds as you like before moving on to another game or some other activity.

One final victory condition that comes to mind is causing a stalemate. You are awarded the victory when your opponent can no longer make a legal move. This is another possible winning condition in *Checkers* (in addition to elimination).

This isn't an exhaustive list, but it should give you some ideas for other possible end game and victory conditions.

Next up, why restrictions are actually a good thing in your game.

ACTION: Think about the current victory and end game conditions for your game. Are they compelling? Do they give players something to strive for? Consider other possible options from this chapter and if any appeal to you, playtest them and get feedback from your playtesters to see if your game has improved.

CHAPTER 31
APPLYING RESTRICTIONS IN YOUR GAME THE RIGHT WAY

"They say that life's a game and then they take the board away."

- Alan Moore, V For Vendetta

Unless you're creating an open sandbox-style game like *Minecraft*, you'll want to consider what types of restrictions players must play within during your game. Still, even with a game like *Minecraft*, players are still restricted by the height, width, and depth of the world and other rules that still apply.

There are times when you'll want to constrict players and other times when you'll want to open up more options for them. A lot depends on the game, the stage of development, and what you're trying to achieve.

So, let's look at when it's a good idea to add more restrictions and when it's a better idea to relax those restrictions.

ADDING RESTRICTIONS

There are so many games that I can think of that impose restrictions on players that make the game more challenging, but at the same time, are completely necessary and definitely make the game better.

For example, in *Azul*, when you take all the tiles of one colour and need to place them on your board, they must all be placed in the same row. You're also unable to place tiles in a row where you've already completed a row of that colour previously.

This can definitely make for some interesting decisions. Also, without such a restriction, players could easily complete one row and start another on the same turn, which might make decisions rather obvious. Instead, you have to decide whether to complete that row you've already started, while taking a penalty, or start an entirely new row, running the risk that you may not complete this either. This definitely makes for a more compelling game.

Allowing players complete free range of movement, placement, and scoring can make it far too easy for players to do whatever they want without having to consider the consequences or other options. It might be fun the first time you play, but you may not return for a second game.

Another good example is *Century Spice Road*. In this engine-building game, once you play a card, it is laid face-down. In order to pick up any cards you've already played, you must take the rest action. You are essentially passing on the opportunity to gain more cards, cubes or score an achievement. If you were able to play the same cards over and over again, it wouldn't be nearly as fun or interesting.

In my co-designed game *14 Frantic Minutes*, I could tell from a very early stage that I needed to add a restriction to avoid the alpha player problem that is so prevalent in many co-op games. *14 Frantic Minutes* is a real-time cooperative puzzle-solving game in which players have polyomino pieces they use to connect circuits. The problem that arose very early in playtesting was that one player could take control or at least leave a quieter player off to the side.

We very much wanted all players to be involved in the game, so we made a change so that each player gets exactly five pieces and only they are allowed to touch them. This ensures that all players contribute and along with the real-time component of the game didn't allow for one player to take over and ruin the fun.

WHEN YOU WANT TO RELAX RESTRICTIONS

At the same time, sometimes you can impose too many constraints in your game. If players complain that they're not able to do everything they'd like to and are feeling too restricted, it might be a good time to take a look at the restrictions you've imposed and see if there are ways to relax them a bit. As long as the changes improve your game, you're heading in the right direction.

I ran into this situation on two different games recently.

I've been working on another co-designed game called *Reef Mates*. This is a game in which players take turns swapping the shark and another creature on the board and then capturing all creatures surrounding the shark that are unprotected. The creatures are laid out randomly at the start of the game, which sometimes results in clumps of creatures of one colour on the board. Since one of the protection conditions is colour, sometimes it would be difficult to break up these groups.

Players were feeling restricted and suggested that rather than creatures of the same colour protecting each other orthogonally and diagonally they should only provide orthogonal protection. I adapted this suggestion and this one tiny rule change improved the game immensely and left players with more interesting options on every turn.

I'm also co-designing a game called *Squirrel Quarrel*. It's a pick-up and deliver game in which you play as a team of squirrels collecting food for the winter. Squirrels take food back to different nests, each with its own reward, but you must keep one of your squirrels on the nest in order to avoid another team's squirrel from taking it over.

The problem was, once you're late in the game, all the squirrels are busy protecting nests and your movement becomes way too restricted. Players end up moving away from the nest to gather something close and then immediately returning on the same turn.

Players really wanted to free up the squirrels so they had more choice. So, for my next playtest any filled nests were scored and placed in front of the player, freeing up that squirrel to help its teammates. I felt that this really opened up gameplay and strategies a lot, making this a much better player experience.

Up next, the 2 types of randomness and how they play a part in your game (and player's perceptions of your game).

ACTION: If you're finding that players have a little too much freedom in your game to do whatever they want and/or choices are too obvious, try implementing some restrictions. Something as simple as a hand limit, a placement rule, or a limit on resources available could take your game from functioning to fantastic.

If you find that players are feeling too constrained and can't do nearly as much as they would like to do and that this is leaving them feeling frustrated rather than having fun, look at ways to open things up a bit. Allow a bit more freedom of movement or a larger hand size and see if this improves the player experience.

CHAPTER 32

THE 2 TYPES OF RANDOMNESS AND HOW TO APPLY THEM TO YOUR GAME

"I learned you can't control everything. You've got to roll with the dice sometimes."

– Anthony Johnson, MMA Fighter

Nobody likes to lose a game because of complete randomness. You want to feel like your decisions matter and that you've either won or lost based on your ability to pull off a particular strategy.

At the same time, creating a game with absolutely no randomness can sometimes lead to a bit of a stale experience. Randomness, done the right way, can actually add a lot of replayability and fun to your board game.

We're going to talk about the two types of randomness, the distinction between the two, and how to apply randomness to your board game in an effective manner. I will also share plenty of examples from board games new and old to help you understand the distinction between the two types of randomness and how other game designers have applied it to their games.

INPUT RANDOMNESS

It can be said that input randomness will help a player to inform their decisions. It's about being put in a situation and then allowing the players to determine their own path.

Essentially, there are one or more things that have been randomized, such as cards, tiles, or tokens, that provide players with different options. This may happen at the start of the game, the beginning of every round, or at different points throughout the game.

For example, think about the tiles that are laid out at the start of each round in *Azul* or the cards available to be purchased in *Splendor*. They have been randomly drawn from a bag or a deck and now players must decide what to do with this random assortment of things in front of them.

When a game does this right, it allows players to see different paths that they may take in order to try to achieve victory. But when it makes choices too obvious, players can see that there is a certain path that is better than others and if they were paying attention, their best move is to take this path.

In general, input randomness is more acceptable to experienced gamers than output randomness and leads to players using their skills more than just luck.

So, let's look now at output randomness and how this differs from input randomness.

OUTPUT RANDOMNESS

With output randomness, on the other hand, your fate is dictated by the roll of a die, draw of a card, or some other action. You have no say in the outcome because it is completely random.

One of the simplest examples of this is flipping a coin. Heads you win, tails you lose.

Imagine playing a game for an hour or two and at the end, you flip a coin to determine whether or not you are the winner. This wouldn't feel very satisfying, would it? You'd wonder why you wasted your evening playing a game where the outcome was determined by a coin flip you could have just made it the start.

However, in some cases, output randomness can bring a lot of excitement to a game.

For example, in *D&D* (*Dungeons and Dragons*), when you attack a creature you roll a die to see if you hit. Then you roll another die to see how much damage you have inflicted. This can lead to some really big moments in a game where you either slay the dragon or trip over your own sword. These memories can last a lifetime.

In other cases, this randomness simply takes away player choice and it feels more like the game is playing you. In *Monopoly*, for example, you often get a double-shot of output randomness. First, you roll the dice and are forced to move exactly that many spaces. There are no alternate paths, no ability to choose between the dice you rolled, and no way to manipulate the dice by even a single pip to make your outcome more favourable. Then, depending on where you land, you may have to draw a card and do whatever it says, pay a fee, or go to jail. If you land on someone else's property, you owe them money.

Just about the only choice you have are whether or not to buy an unowned property you land on and whether or not to put up houses or hotels on your own properties (and these decisions are mostly dependent on whether you have enough money to afford them).

So, you can see that output randomness in certain circumstances can lead to some wonderful experiences in some cases, however, much of the time it can feel more like the game is playing you.

HOW TO APPLY RANDOMNESS WELL IN YOUR OWN GAME

When applying randomness to your own game, the first thing you'll want to do is determine what type of experience you want your players to have. Do you want outcomes determined by luck or skillful play? Do you want big swingy moments in your game or more predictability?

Asking yourself these types of questions will help you understand how best to proceed.

Allowing players to make random draws or select from random objects (possibly with replacement as options are taken), allows them to develop a strategy over time. They have to react to what is presented and make the best choice or choose which direction to go. However, this may also open up "hate drafting." That is, players select something not because it helps them but because they know another player wants this and they want to deny them. So, it's helpful to see how this plays out through extensive playtesting and getting feedback.

Just keep in mind that too little choice may lead to obvious decisions, whereas too much choice can lead to analysis paralysis (AP). I find that providing players with 3-5 choices usually works well in many games, however, this is dependent on the game and how flexible or rigid you want to be.

Next up, we'll talk about more about determining the winner of your game and how to handle a tie.

ACTION: It's good to return to the vision for your game when you're making decisions about changes and possible mechanics to use. You want the actual player experience to match what you have intended. Sometimes that may require either input or output randomness depending on the game.

However, I would recommend that you generally stick to input randomness to create challenges for players and add to the replayability over output randomness, which often leads to more luck-based outcomes.

CHAPTER 33

WHY NOBODY LIKES TIES AND HOW TO BREAK TIES IN YOUR GAME

"Money isn't everything, but it is a tiebreaker in Power Grid."

- Unknown

In the previous chapter, I talked about why nobody likes to lose a game because of complete randomness and how to apply randomness to your game the right way. In this chapter, we're going to look at the reason that many players don't like to end a game in a tie and what you can do to break ties and help determine a winner in any situation.

You've been moving your pawn around, gathering resources and picking up just the right cards, and have pulled off your strategy. However, another player also found success with their own unique strategy and after playing the game for an hour or two, the game ended in a tie. That's not a very satisfactory feeling at the end of a game. Of course, you'd like to come out the victor, but even if you don't, it's often better to have one player declared the winner.

If you're a competitive player, it can feel like you've just wasted a good deal of time and have not come any closer to declaring who the better player is, at least this time around.

In sports, a tie is said to be like kissing your sister. While I don't necessarily share this exact sentiment, it's understandable that many sports have employed the use of overtime or even a shootout to declare a winner. During the regular season, there may be the opportunity for ties, but when it comes to the playoffs, one team must always advance and only a single team can be crowned the champion.

However, there are ways to break ties that are fair and rational, and others that don't leave either anyone feeling satisfied. So, let's look at some ways to break ties effectively and ways you should avoid doing so.

TIEBREAKERS TO AVOID

Nobody wants to play a one hour game where the winner is determined by the flip of a coin. That hardly seems fair.

It may seem obvious, but you don't want to break a tie through something like flipping a coin or rolling a die and declaring the player who rolled higher as the winner. So, make sure to avoid creating a tiebreaker that will be based completely on luck (unless your game itself is completely luck-based).

You'll also want to avoid tiebreakers that don't fall in line with the theme or require an additional component just to determine the winner. Rather, a tiebreaker should be in line with the gameplay and what players are striving to do throughout the game.

HOW TO CREATE A FAIR TIEBREAKER

The first thing you want to do when determining what to use as a tiebreaker in your game is to think about what you are incentivizing your players to do.

If you are trying to get players to play as efficiently as possible, then a good tiebreaker may be the player who has accomplished their score with the fewest cards or has the fewest resources remaining.

If your game is about accumulating a lot of resources, that tie could be broken by the player with the most of a certain type of resource collected.

If your game is a race to the finish, you might want to consider something along the lines of how many items a player has collected or how much fuel they have remaining.

Or you might want to break the tie by declaring the player with the most bonus points or private goal cards accomplished.

It might even be based on the player who went first, last, or made the most progress on a specific track.

Your tiebreaker really depends on what your game is about and what players do from one turn to the next. Try to keep your tiebreaker thematic and in line with what you want players to do in your game.

Some games employ multiple tie-breaking conditions, as it could be quite possible that players could tie not only with the most points, but also with the most gold, silver, etc, and will need multiple conditions in order to determine a victor. However, you'll want to avoid creating a laundry list of tiebreaking conditions that require players to spend a lot of time counting all the resources at the end of the game. At some point, you'll probably have to say that if a tie still remains, the players share the victory. If it is determined that two players actually did play equally well on all fronts, they will usually be able to accept that they are both victors.

Although I've yet to play this, I understand that the tiebreaker in *Arboretum* is stated as, "If there is still a tie, the players must each plant a tree. In 5 years' time, the player whose tree has grown the tallest wins." I think that's a pretty cool way to handle a tie!

"So, is my game done now?" you ask. You're about to find out.

ACTION: The best advice for creating a tiebreaker in your game is to keep it thematic and in line with what you expect players to do in your game. Quite often this will be based on the most resources of one type, particularly something that is valuable in your game, however, this will be highly dependent on what players are trying to accomplish.

SECTION 6

FINISHING YOUR GAME
(HOW TO KNOW IT'S DONE)

CHAPTER 34
KNOWING WHEN YOUR GAME IS DONE

"You must know what your audience will and will not like, and you must know it even better than they do. You would think that finding out what people want would be easy, but it isn't, because in many cases, they don't really know. They might think they know, but often there is a big difference between what they think they want and what it is they will actually enjoy."

- Jesse Schell, The Art of Game Design: A Book of Lenses

One of the toughest challenges board game designers face is knowing whether their game is done. "Done", as mentioned, is a tricky term. What we're referring to is the point at which you can't do much more to improve upon it. We previously spoke about how to know your game is ready for unguided playtesting, which is also a pretty good indication that your game is nearing completion.

Once you've run a number of successful unguided tests and feel that your game is really consistent and engaging, you'll know that you're in the home stretch. In this chapter, we'll build on the unguided playtesting criteria and go through the checklist to know when you're nearing completion.

VERY LITTLE FEEDBACK FOR IMPROVEMENT

By this point, playtesters are likely to be giving you very little feedback for ways to improve your game. Very few issues should arise. The only suggestions they may offer will be around making your game a bit different, but not necessarily better. Your game should be playing consistently, with players being fully engaged, and really enjoying the experience.

CONSISTENT EXPERIENCE

If your unguided playtests have gone over well, meaning that players understand the game consistently, new players aren't running into any major issues, and rules are clear and being followed correctly, then your game is nearly there. As long as no major issues are being identified, your expectations have been met for the vision, experience, and feel you set out to accomplish, you're one step closer to sharing your game with the world.

Also, if players are asking to play again or buy your game right then and there, you know you're on the right track!

AIM FOR DONE, NOT PERFECT

Many people are perfectionists, and board game designers are no exception. I once thought of myself as a perfectionist, but over time I came to realize that perfection is the enemy of really great. In reality, perfection is actually unattainable.

You could keep iterating your game forever, making minor improvements and little tweaks here and there, however you must understand the law of diminishing return. At first when you make changes to your game it can go through some major improvements, however you'll get to the point where all the hours you put in to making changes will make very little improvement to your game.

One of the biggest risks with aiming for perfection is that you will never finish what you set out to accomplish. That would be an incredible shame. You have to realize that your game will never be perfect, and this doesn't matter because there will be people out there who will love to play your game. Let's get this done so you can share it with the world!

No matter what, someone will always find an issue or complain about some aspect of your game. You have to realize that you can't please everyone. You can definitely minimize these issues, but you must also understand that your game will not be perfect. There's no such thing as the perfect game. Just make sure that the group you are targeting is the appropriate audience and that you've made a really great game for them.

Some game designers joke that they know their game is done when they're tired of it and never want to see it again. Now while this is funny, there's definitely a grain of truth to it. By this point you will have played your game so many times, that you may actually be sick of it. As long as others don't feel the same way though, you're still good!

What you want to do is take your game as far as you can by yourself. Sometimes it's then necessary to bring in a developer to take it that last mile, whether this is done by the publisher that signed your game or by you if you have decided to self-publish.

IF YOU GO THROUGH A TRADITIONAL PUBLISHER, THEY WILL FINISH IT

You also have to be aware that if your game is picked up by a publisher, they will own the rights to it, and they can (and will) change it as they please. So even though you feel that your game is really polished, they will ultimately control its destiny.

I'm going to share with you now my top 5 ways to know your game is ready to pitch or publish. However, if you're self-publishing, note that this is referring to your game being done, not that you're ready to launch, which require a whole lot more work.

#5 THE FEEDBACK YOU'RE RECEIVING WOULD MAKE THE GAME DIFFERENT BUT NOT BETTER

When you playtest your game with other designers and players, you'll often receive a lot of feedback. Quite often it will be necessary criticism that you need to hear in order to identify problems with your game and make it the best it can be.

Often, other designers will give you feedback that would change the game more into the game that they would have designed or would have liked to play, so you have to watch for this.

But when players only have suggestions on how to make small changes that would make the game slightly different, but not necessarily better, take note of this. If this is the only feedback you're consistently receiving and there are no major problems being identified and no suggestions for improving your game, this is a great sign.

#4 PLAYERS WANT TO IMMEDIATELY PLAY AGAIN

"Can we play again?"

This is like music to a game designer's ears.

While this won't happen with every game, particularly longer games that you wouldn't normally play multiple times in a row, with a shorter game, this is something you want to hear from your players. If one player has just tasted defeat, they may want a re-match. If it's a co-op game and the players narrowly lost, they may want another chance at redemption.

If your game is a bit on the longer side, what you might hear instead is players discussing strategy and what they would do the next time they play. They've found some depth to your game and have indicated they are interested in playing again in the future.

If you're hearing any of these types of comments consistently, you can be confident that your game is getting close to the stage where you'll be ready to pitch it to publishers.

#3 PUBLISHERS PLAYING YOUR GAME GIVE YOU THEIR CARD AND ASK YOU YOUR PLANS

If you have the opportunity to play your game with one or more publishers, do it! They are a wealth of information and can often give you great feedback about the gameplay, rules, and how to look at your game as not just a game, but also as a product.

If you're really fortunate and a publisher takes a liking to your game, they may want to pursue it further. If it complements their catalogue and they can see it being a potential addition to their line-up, they might give you their card and ask you what you plan to do with your game.

You may even end up getting your game signed as a result (just don't expect this to happen on the spot!).

#2 PLAYERS ASK WHEN YOUR GAME IS COMING OUT AND HOW THEY CAN FIND OUT ABOUT THIS

If players finish playing your game and immediately ask when it will be available, this is a great sign. It's even better if they say this *while* playing your game.

They've indicated they enjoyed your game and are interested in picking it up when it becomes available.

If your players are consistently asking when your game is coming out, it means there is some demand for it, which is always a great thing!

#1 PEOPLE WANT TO BUY YOUR GAME RIGHT NOW!

It's an amazing feeling when someone is ready to pull out their credit card and buy your game right there on the spot.

If players are asking to buy your game right now, they are putting their money where their mouth is. They're not just saying they like your game, they are ready to put down their hard-earned cash to get a copy so that they can share this with their friends and family.

If this is happening consistently, there is definitely a demand for your game and there is something special about it. You're now ready to pitch that game to a publisher (and you can even mention/share a list of people who want to buy it right now)!

GAME COMPLETION CHECKLIST

Run through the checklist below and see if you can honestly check off each of these boxes. If they are all complete, you should be good to go!

- Your game plays well consistently without any interaction on your part

- The rules are clear and are followed correctly and consistently

- New players can easily understand your game without any issues

- The art and graphic design match your theme well

- The vision and experience/feel you intended for the game is consistently felt by players

- Feedback is consistently positive with no significant suggestions for improvement

Next up, we'll make sure your game looks as good as it plays!

ACTION: Determine if your game is "done" by using the checklist in this chapter. If so, it's time to put the finishing touches on your game and determine your next steps. If not, make sure to continue playtesting and improving your game until all the criteria are met, so you can take one step closer to sharing your game with the world.

CHAPTER 35
ART/DESIGN/LAYOUT (LOOK AND FEEL)

"An artist is someone who takes you where you could never go alone."

- Jesse Schell, The Art of Game Design: A Book of Lenses

Art and graphic design are two distinct things. Both will be required for your game, and you are often best off hiring a separate graphic designer to work on the format and layout of your files and materials, and an artist to provide you with all the artwork for your game.

You may be tempted to hire an artist to do everything, but if this individual is not familiar with graphic design, you might get into trouble. Graphic artists will understand how to lay out files for printing, ensuring the bleed lines are set correctly, and that everything will print properly. Conversely, a graphic designer may not be able to create the thematic art you are looking for.

I am very fortunate to have found a great graphic designer/artist, Tristam Rossin, who has become a friend as well. He put together all the art and graphic design for *Relics of Rajavihara* and the expansion *Montalo's Revenge*, as well as *14 Frantic Minutes*. However, not everyone will be so versatile.

A good graphic designer with lots of experience will understand file layouts and should be able to design exactly what you need. He or she can also work directly with your printing and manufacturing company to ensure that everything is done correctly, as well as fix any issues that might arise.

WHAT YOU NEED DEPENDS ON YOUR GOAL

If you decide to self-publish, your art and design need to be quite different than what would be required to pitch to a publisher. When self-publishing, whether using crowdfunding, selling directly, or a Print-on-Demand service, you will be the one paying for this. Everything will remain under your control, and it will ultimately be your decision who you work with and what gets used in your game.

You will want to find a talented, reliable, experienced artist, along with a good, experienced graphic designer. Since you will be publishing this yourself, you'll want to ensure everything is high quality and worth the money you spend. The art and visual appeal of your page can make or break your Kickstarter campaign.

If you're planning on going with a traditional publisher, you're going to approach art and graphic design much differently. If you find a publisher who is interested in your game, you will be providing them with a prototype, which will include a rough idea of the art and layout you want to use in your game. What you want to use here is simply "placeholder art", as the publisher will have the ultimate say about what the game will actually look like. They will be the one to choose the artist, who may work in-house or as a freelancer.

The publisher may ask for your input on this and other aspects of your game, but they are not required to. Make sure not to spend money on art and graphic design if you are taking this route, as the publisher will decide on this. Instead, use whatever Google images or royalty-free art you can find that goes well with the theme and conveys your player experience.

MAKE SURE THE ART AND DESIGN IS CONSISTENT WITH YOUR THEME

Whichever route you take, you want to make sure that the art and graphic design is a logical match with the theme and gameplay. It should enhance the experience, making players feel more a part of the game and the world in which it takes place. Ensure that this flows seamlessly and makes your game an even more enjoyable experience.

VISUALLY APPEALING

It should go without saying that the art in your game should be striking and get people's attention. Just saying you should have beautiful art is a challenge though because this is subjective. What you want to do is make sure that the art will be perceived as beautiful by the audience that will be playing your game and well-matched to the theme.

The art and style should also be appropriate for your game. If your game is meant for kids with a very family-friendly theme, you may want to aim for cartoonish, fun, or quirky - whatever you feel appeals to families. However, if you are creating a dungeon crawler, your art and design should be reflective of the monsters and creatures you are creating, and convey feelings of dread and challenge.

Munchkin for example, uses light, funny art, as this game is meant to be comical. On the other hand, *Dixit*, a great party game, utilizes beautiful and sometimes abstract art (with different artists for each deck), which players have to interpret and choose from based on clues given by other players.

If possible, you want your game to look really unique and stand out. With the number of games being produced today, anything that can make people stop and stare has a serious advantage. It's often helpful to share your images and designs in board game designer groups online to get other people's opinions. You can even get members to vote between single pieces of art provided by multiple artists to help you determine who you should hire or what direction you should go. This may also lead to more interest in your game without having to resort to self-promotion.

MAKE SURE THE DESIGN IS EASY TO FOLLOW

While you want to make sure the art and design are beautiful, unique, and get people's attention, everything also has to be functional. Ensure that the art is consistent through the game. The design should be such that it is legible and easy to follow. Icons and symbols can and should be used, but make sure they are used consistently.

The design should also lead players seamlessly through the game, whether it be through the action steps on cards, player movement on the board, the outline of the rules, player reference cards, or any other aspect of your game.

WHERE TO FIND ARTISTS & GRAPHIC DESIGNERS

There are a number of places you can find board game artists and graphic designers. Search online and look in forums on Boardgamegeek, Facebook, and elsewhere. You can also find profiles on Gamecrafter and other artist websites.

You'll also see lots of great artistic renderings on social media. Just have a look around to find something you like.

When you discover an artist or artists you may like to work with, reach out to them to let them know about your project and try to determine if you will be a good fit for each other. Make sure that everything you agree upon is written up in a contract, so that each party is aware of their responsibilities. You may want to start with a sample piece and see if that artist can create what you're looking for.

Up next, we'll talk about getting your prototype made so you can sell your game to a publisher and retire rich (hey, we can always dream, right?).

ACTION: The next steps will depend on the goal for your game. If you're pitching to a publisher, make sure the layout and art is appealing and matches well with the vision, but don't spend money on this.

If you plan on self-publishing, look for an appropriate artist (or artists) and a good graphic designer. Hire people who do good work, are easy to work with, and will deliver. They must be able to convey your vision well, so make sure you choose wisely.

CHAPTER 36
PROTOTYPING

"Play is to be played exactly because it isn't serious; it frees us from seriousness."

- Michael Novak, The Joy of Sports

By this point you will have a game that should be functioning well, and provides a consistently fun and engaging experience for players. It may or may not look as polished as a game you would find on the shelf, so you are probably ready for the next step, which is creating a solid prototype of your game.

WELL, THAT DEPENDS...

As with a lot of decisions you have to make with your game, much of this comes down once again to how you plan on publishing your game, whether through self-publishing or a traditional publisher.

If you're self-publishing, you'll want to put a lot more time and effort into creating a really nice-looking prototype. You want this to be visually appealing and really professional, as this will show your potential customers you are serious about making a great-looking game.

They always say, "don't judge a book by its cover," and you could say the same thing about not judging a game by its box, however in most cases this will be the first thing that people see. People may also see the game set up and being played by other players, so making a good first impression is very important.

You want to make sure to wait until your game is really complete before you spend time and money on a good-looking prototype. It's a big pain (and cost) to have prototypes made all over again after making a significant change to your game, so make sure you're ready.

For your prototype, you'll want to include the box, board, cards, and all components (depending on what your game entails). You may also decide to get the printing done and add in your own components that you already have on hand from playtesting.

If you're self-publishing, the main reason you'll want good-looking prototypes is to have them available for reviewers, your promo video, Cons, and other events. If a reviewer has agreed to do a video review of your game (or even a written review), you want them to be able to display a really eye-catching product. This can go a long way to showing your game in a positive light.

On the other hand, if you're going to be going through a traditional publisher, your prototype doesn't necessarily have to be quite as polished. However, a good-looking prototype can help get a publisher's attention. At the very least, you'll want to have a good, playable version of your game.

Make sure that you provide everything needed to play your game. Avoid sending publishers a PDF that they will need to print, cut up, and assemble, unless they request this. In many cases they just don't have the time to do this. Still, you should have a PDF print and play ready in case they do ask. Otherwise, give them a good physical copy, including the rules and all components needed so that they can play the game on their own.

WHERE TO GET THIS DONE

You can always create your prototype yourself, especially if you are going to be pitching to a publisher. You can create a basic but decent version, including all the components and parts needed to play your game. You may be able to print everything yourself, or get some help if you have a friend or colleague who can assist you with the design. Put everything together in a nice-looking box and you'll be ready to share this with others.

However, you're more likely to want to get some professional help with your prototype. There are a number of companies that can do this for you, and you can usually get an online quote directly from their website. That way you will know the exact cost to get the parts you need made, and at what quantities, along with the cost and timing for shipping.

You'll want to look for printers that specialize in small print runs rather than those with higher minimum orders such as 500, 1,000, or 2,000 copies, which is typical for these larger manufacturers. You may want to get 5-10 copies or more depending on the purpose. You will probably want to have at least a few copies to ship out to reviewers if you're self-publishing, plus more copies to take to Cons and other events. Or, if you've given yourself and your reviewers plenty of time before your campaign (which you should aim for), you can ask one reviewer to pass on their copy to another reviewer, with you covering the shipping costs.

I suggest leaning towards more copies rather than less, since you'll have to pay shipping again if you have to make a second order. You may also save money by ordering a slightly larger quantity. Also, if you have reviewers already lined up, you can save some money by having them sent directly to the reviewers rather than first to you, then you having to ship to the reviewer.

You may choose to just have certain aspects of your game printed, such as good-quality cards, and add any other components yourself. You may be able to get your own boxes and print off your own cover for the box as well.

There are a number of good services available online. Here are just a few of them:

The Gamecrafter – These guys pretty much do it all. They have boxes, boards, cards, and almost any component you can think of. They also offer a Print-on-Demand service. Most of the components I have in my collection are from The Gamecrafter.

Drive-Thru Cards – They produce high-quality stuff, but only cards.

Printer Studio – They focus mostly on cards. I have used Printer Studio for a card game prototype and was impressed by the quality.

Print & Play – This is a small division of Ad Magic, who are known for producing Cards Against Humanity and Exploding Kittens, among other games.

Boardgamesmaker – This company provides custom components and can also print your cards, boards, boxes, etc.

With the rise in popularity of board gaming, new options are always popping up. Make sure to look online for other resources as well.

There you have it. Your game is now done. Congratulations! In the next section we'll go over all the options you have available to share your game with the world so that you can make the best decision for your situation.

ACTION: Based on how you decide to move forward with your game, decide on who you want to print your prototype, or if you will do this yourself. You may need help with the graphic design here to get it right (file layout, etc.). Make sure to get enough copies printed for your purposes, such as reviewers, pitching, events, and copies to have on hand just in case.

SECTION 7

NOW THAT YOUR GAME IS DONE (WHAT'S NEXT?)

CHAPTER 37
CHOICES/OPTIONS

"The really blisteringly original games are incredibly simple."

- Paul Reiche III, game designer

As previously mentioned, there are a number of different options you can choose from once your game is done. I will go into a lot more detail on each of these choices in this section.

THERE'S NO RIGHT ANSWER

No one option is necessarily better than the others, they're just different. You have to choose the one that's right for you.

Whatever you choose is really up to you. No judgment. I just want to be able to provide you with as much information as I can, so you can make an informed decision and know exactly what each one entails. It really is good to understand all options available, so I strongly urge you to read this entire section. It may end up changing the course you take, as you will have a better appreciation for the risks and benefits of each approach.

Also note that you don't necessarily have to use the same method for every game you create. With some games you may be confident self-publishing them, while others you may be more comfortable having a publisher handle. Or you may go with an entirely different approach.

YOU HAVE OPTIONS

Ultimately, there are a few choices you have when it comes to the next step you take with your game:

- Pitch to publishers (the traditional approach)

- Self-publishing (either directly, or through a crowdfunding platform such as Kickstarter, Gamefound, Backerkit, Game On Tabletop, etc.)

- An alternative approach such as Print-on-Demand, Print and Play, or just enjoying your game with friends and family

Below is a summary chart outlining these options. This discusses some of the details along with pros and cons of each approach. These all refer to the point at which your game is "done" and are based on typical situations. This of course varies depending on the game and how well everything is planned. This is by no means a substitute for all the crucial details you'll need to know that we'll get into the next few chapters, but it will give you a decent starting point when considering your options.

TRADITIONAL PUBLISHER

- **Capital Investment:** Minimal

- **Time to Get to Market Once Done:** Long (approx. 1-3 years)

- **Creative Control:** Given up

- **Distribution (# of Games):** Highest (approx. 5,000-10,000+)

- **Risk:** Low

- **Time Investment:** Low to Medium

- **Marketing:** Publisher

- **Expected $:** Royalty payments differ, typically in the range of 2-10% of net sales

- **Biggest Benefits:** They do the business work, so you can focus on game design; little risk

- **Biggest Drawbacks:** You lose creative control; game may change considerably; game may not get published; reliance on publisher to market game; you only receive a small portion of the profit

SELF-PUBLISHING DIRECTLY

- **Capital Investment:** High

- **Time to Get to Market Once Done:** Reasonably short (aprox. 3-6 months)

- **Creative Control:** Completely yours

- **Distribution (# of Games):** Low (based on your expected demand and investment)

- **Risk:** High

- **Time Investment:** High

- **Marketing:** You

- **Expected $:** Depends on sales (could make or lose a lot of money)

- **Biggest Benefits:** You maintain complete control; this option has the highest financial upside if your game is really successful

- **Biggest Drawbacks:** A lot of work; investing your own money; demand unknown; have to market on your own

SELF-PUBLISHING THROUGH CROWDFUNDING

- **Capital Investment:** Moderate to high

- **Time to Get to Market Once Done:** Moderate (approx 4-12+ months)

- **Creative Control:** Mostly yours, with backer input

- **Distribution (# of Games):** Low (1,000-2,000+ if successful)

- **Risk:** Low-Medium

- **Time Investment:** High

- **Marketing:** You

- **Expected $:** Depends on funding (if well-planned, should at least break even if successfully funded) and next steps

- **Biggest Benefits:** You maintain control; only produce if funded; allows you to gauge demand; big financial upside if your game is really successful

- **Biggest Drawbacks:** A lot of work; some investment needed; keeping backers happy; only a starting point and need to determine next steps

PRINT-ON-DEMAND

- **Capital Investment:** Minimal

- **Time to Get to Market Once Done:** Very short

- **Creative Control:** Completely yours

- **Distribution (# of Games):** Very Low (<1,000)

- **Risk:** Low

- **Time Investment:** Low

- **Marketing:** You

- **Expected $:** Minimal

- **Biggest Benefits:** You maintain creative control; minimal investment; only purchased games printed (no guessing about demand); more time for game design

- **Biggest Drawbacks:** Little monetary gain expected; very little exposure to market

PRINT AND PLAY

- **Capital Investment:** Minimal

- **Time to Get to Market Once Done:** Immediate

- **Creative Control:** Completely yours

- **Distribution (# of Games):** Very Low (<1,000)

- **Risk:** Low

- **Time Investment:** Low

- **Marketing:** You

- **Expected $:** Minimal

- **Biggest Benefits:** You maintain creative control; no cost; more time for game design

- **Biggest Drawbacks:** No monetary gain expected; most people not interested in the work involved to put together your game

Now, with this information we're ready to jump right into these options in more detail to help you decide which is best for you, and how to improve your odds of success.

ACTION: Based on the information in this chapter, determine which routes appeal to you the most and which ones you will most likely want to avoid. Read on, making sure that you take the time to go over all the chapters in this section, even if you are completely sure of your next step. It's best to know all your available options, as well as the pros and cons of each approach, so you can choose the best one for you and your current game.

CHAPTER 38
PITCHING TO PUBLISHERS (TRADITIONAL)

"Early on, I figured out that I just want to design games. I don't want to be a publisher. I'm not seeking employment in the industry. And I most certainly don't want to run crowdfunding campaigns to self-publish. You need to know what role you want to play in the field. If you don't commit to something specific, you may find yourself trying to do everything, then struggling to make it happen, and struggling to do it well."

– Luke Laurie, co-designer of Manhattan Project: Energy Empire

Up until recently, if you created a board game and wanted to share it with the world, unless you were willing to risk a lot of your own money, your only option was to have it picked up by a board game publisher. However, this was becoming increasingly more difficult as there were only a small number of major players, and many of them were not accepting pitches from the public. There were very few other smaller publishers, and some of them were getting eaten up by the publishing giants. Also, when Hasbro bought out Parker Brothers and Milton Bradley (who were both huge in the board game industry), they became the dominant publisher.

But things have changed, and many small publishers have emerged on the scene. Nowadays, designers have many more options than ever. However, depending on your goals, going the traditional route of pitching to a publisher may still be right for you.

FIRST, THE PROS

There are a lot of benefits to having a publisher produce your game, that is, if you are lucky enough to have one interested in signing it. Many publishers get hundreds (if not thousands) of submissions and may only have a few game releases each year.

But if a publisher does release your game, the great thing is, they will do all the heavy lifting, including getting the game manufactured, marketed, and into the big retail stores and/or game shops where people can easily find them. By not having to worry about these responsibilities, you can focus your time on designing more games.

You can also expect a larger print run and more reach, especially with larger publishers, as they will often do a print run of 5,000 to 10,000 games or more, with the possibility of additional print runs if there's enough demand. A typical game successfully funded on Kickstarter on the other hand may only generate a print run of 1,000 to 2,000 games. For a self-publisher, this is considered pretty successful. It's clear that your game will usually get much more exposure by working with a publisher, plus you will get royalties for every copy sold.

NOW, THE CONS

There are some downsides to traditional publishing though. One of the big ones is the loss of creative control. Once you sign over your game to a publisher, they have the right to change the theme, mechanics, and even the name of your game. If maintaining creative control over your vision is the most important thing to you, this may not be ideal.

There's also a chance that your game will never see the light of day. The timing may be off, or they may just choose to go a different direction, leaving your game on the shelf for an extended period of time.

Also, don't expect to make a ton of money. Unless your game becomes the next *Ticket to Ride* or *Catan*, you probably won't be retiring anytime soon.

A WORD ABOUT PUBLISHERS

Today, there are a lot of options for different publishers you can work with. They range from the market-dominating Hasbro (estimated at somewhere between 50-80% of market share), to other large companies like Asmodee and Ravensburger, to small publishers like Stonemaier Games and Smirk & Dagger, to self-publishers who have run just one Kickstarter campaign. Some are toy and game companies, while others focus solely on board games.

What's important to note is that not all publishers accept outside submissions. Companies like Funko Games work only with an in-house development team, while some other big publishers may only team up with agents they've worked with in the past. To get your game in front of them, you'll have to work with a recognized agent, who may take 30-60% of your cut on royalties should your game be signed. This could be worth it for the potential high volume of sales this could generate, but that's for you to decide. Other companies may either design most games themselves or have so many games lined up in their queue that they are not accepting submissions at a particular time.

If you do sign on with a larger publisher, you may expect to wait a fairly long time, up to two or three years before you see your game on the shelf. Other smaller publishers, especially those who rely on Kickstarter campaigns to launch their board games, may be totally focused on your game alone and will be able to get it to the market much faster.

What's important is to find a publisher that's a good match for you. You'll want to find a publisher that is not only easy to work with, but who is also interested in your specific type of game. For example, it doesn't make sense to pitch a party game to a publisher that only produces war games. Make sure you know what games publishers would love to see.

You'll also want to look at what games a publisher already has on the market. If your game is too similar to one of theirs, they may not be interested in having this compete directly with an existing game.

Do your research and narrow down your list to a small number of publishers who you think might be interested in your game. One great resource you can use here is the Cardboard Edison Compendium. This listing includes hundreds of publishers and details such as the types of games they produce, if they are currently accepting submissions, as well as contact information. You can get access to this resource, which they keep updated, at a very low cost and it is well worth the small investment.

THE PROCESS (TYPICALLY)

Although each publisher and designer interaction will be slightly different, the process for pitching to a publisher typically is as follows:

- Meet/contact

- Provide a sell sheet

- If the publisher is interested, they may ask for the rulebook, a short video or may want to set up a demo meeting at an upcoming convention

- The publisher may request a prototype

- If interested, the publisher may require more time to playtest, and may even pay you for the right to hold onto it longer than initially expected

- If the publisher wants to publish your game, they will present you with a contract, which you may negotiate, sign, or decline

- The production may take between one to three years (depending on the size of publisher and games in their queue) and will involve playtesting, development, art, and design, etc.

- Depending on the publisher and your own interest, they may involve you in certain aspects of the project

- If all goes well, your game will be published and will be available in retail stores (or on Kickstarter if the publisher uses this method)

- You will be paid royalties on each copy of the game sold based on your agreement

- The pay schedule may vary from publisher to publisher, so you could receive royalties once, twice, or four times per year

- Expect there to be a delay from the time your game is published until you receive any of these royalties

- If your game is a big success, they may decide to do additional print runs

HOW TO APPROACH A PUBLISHER

How does this all sound to you? Are you thinking of pitching your game to a publisher? If so, my advice is to be professional and respectful when talking with a publisher. Develop a reputation as a great designer and someone who is easy to work with. The board game community may seem large, but it's really a small world. You don't want to burn any bridges or get a bad reputation.

You want to have a solid elevator pitch. Be able to describe in 30 seconds or less what your game is about and the "hook" that makes it unique and interesting. Get their attention by practicing this and having it down cold.

Never approach a publisher saying, "my game is going to be the next *Monopoly*." They've heard this too many times before. Besides, the world doesn't need another *Monopoly*. If a publisher is not interested in your game, avoid telling them, "you'll be sorry," or anything along those lines. They receive hundreds of pitches each year and can't possibly produce every game they see, even if they think it has potential. They need to prioritize and focus on a small number of game designs they feel will be successful.

Also, never ask publishers to sigh a non-disclosure agreement (NDA). Publishers aren't trying to steal your idea, and if you push for this, no publisher will be interested. First off, they may already have a similar idea in the works. Secondly, they may have been burned in the past using this approach and don't want to go through this experience again. Having said that, some larger publishers may ask you to sign an NDA, which is totally fine. It mostly protects them in the instance that you pitch something similar to another game they already have in the pipeline.

PERSONALIZE IT!

Make sure to be personal in your approach. When you're contacting a publisher, rather than send a generic letter, personalize it. If possible, find out your contact person's name and address this to them, rather than "to whom it may concern." Know your stuff. Talk about other games the publisher has made that you love, why you want to work with them, and why your game will fit well with and complement their existing catalogue.

You may be asking "should I approach one single publisher or a number of them?" This is a really good question. Either approach can be taken, however I encourage you to let publishers know when you contact them if you are also approaching other publishers, just so they are aware. This is the respectful thing to do.

The process of reviewing your submission, reading your rules, or watching your video and getting back to you can take a while. So, it can be more efficient time-wise to approach multiple publishers at once rather than waiting to see each publisher's response before talking to others. However, if one asks for a prototype, it's best to only send one to them, and put all other subsequent requests on hold until something is decided.

One common and easy approach for contacting publishers is cold emailing them, or filling in a submission form on their website. For each publisher, check the details on their website to see if they are accepting submissions and how they like to be approached, then follow these steps. They will also likely provide details on the types of games they are interested in seeing on their site. Some publishers don't accept outside submissions, so if you find this out, move on to the next one.

Remember that they are very busy and receive a lot of submissions, so don't expect an immediate reply. If a couple of weeks pass, it's perfectly reasonable to contact them to see how everything is proceeding.

DEVELOP A RELATIONSHIP

A more effective way to pitch to publishers is to first develop a relationship. But how do you do this? Well, one way is to interact with them online. If they have a blog or forum, be active on it. If they recognize your name, there's a higher chance they will look at your email and hopefully, your game.

You may also have the opportunity to meet publishers at prototype events or conventions. This is a great way to network and get your name out there. You can even volunteer to help a publishing company at a convention. They quite often need help demoing games or manning booths, and this is a good way to get your foot in the door.

If someone helped you out with something and did a great job, wouldn't you be more willing to look at an idea they had and give them feedback? Even if they don't have any interest in signing your game, publishers can give you some really helpful advice on how to make your game even better, or even recommend another publisher that might be interested. Remember, they have a lot of experience and know what sells.

Some conventions and get-togethers also include a Publisher Speed Dating event. This is a rapid-paced opportunity to pitch your game (or games) to a number of publishers. Typically, a publisher will sit down at your table, and you'll have about five minutes to talk about your game. Then they will take a few minutes to give you feedback, and may take your sell sheet if they are interested. Next, publishers will rotate, and the process continues. These events are usually one to two hours long and give you some great opportunities to work on your pitch and presentation, along with gaining some valuable insights. There is also the possibility that a publisher may be interested in hearing more about your game or even sign it right there!

SELL SHEETS

I strongly suggest you create a sell sheet for your game. This is a one-page sheet that explains what your game is all about and can be emailed to publishers or given to them in person. On your sell sheet, make sure to include how to play your game, images, demographics (age range, play time, number of players), components, the hook, and of course your contact information. Make it visually appealing, not too wordy, and ensure that the reader will have a good basic understanding of how the game works (a quick example turn can help here) without doing a full rules explanation.

Curt Covert at Smirk & Dagger also talks about the "golden moment" in a game, where something happens that causes a big reaction. This is another great thing you can either include in your sell sheet or discuss with publishers when talking about your game.

Check out a great example of a sell sheet from the Bamboozle Brothers in the resource section of this book.

You'll also want to make sure your rules sheet or rule book is clear and concise. Publishers may also request this in order to better understand your game.

In addition, publishers may be interested in seeing a short play through video, in which you introduce yourself, the game, and show how it's played. It's best to keep this to under five minutes if possible. The shorter, the better.

By this point you should also have a good-looking prototype. It's great to have copies of your prototype at conventions and other events, and some on hand to send to publishers if they're interested, but never, under any circumstances should you send this directly to a publisher unless you've been asked to send them your game. If you send this before it is requested, you'll be wasting time and money, as your game will be unopened and may not even be returned to you.

Remember that just because a publisher is interested in your game, it doesn't mean you have to sign with them. Much like a job interview, you may be offered a position, but if it isn't exactly what you're looking for or you don't think that the company will be a good fit, you can always say no. Sure, it would be great to see a game on the shelf with your name on it, but you want to be happy with the process and who you are working with. If your game is really good, you'll find a great publisher who wants to work with you.

I've had four games published with different publishers at this point, in addition to the games that I have self-published. I've also had plenty of rejections. And I'm fine with this. It's a bit of a numbers game. Publishers see hundreds of games every year and most only publish a few, so the odds are that most games will be passed on.

It's all part of the process and I've learned from each experience and have become a better designer as a result. At the same time, I've also developed good relationships with many publishers, which makes it much easier to approach them again when I have a new game in the works. Think about this as sowing the seeds for future opportunities.

If you do sign with a publisher, there will be many things you'll want to consider, and you'll want to ensure that all the details are very clear. Beyond the monetary considerations (which will include the agreed upon royalty rate, pay schedule, and possible up-front advances against royalties, etc.), there are some other aspects you will be interested in clarifying in the contract:

How long can the publisher hold onto your game before releasing this back to you (in case they decide not to move ahead with it, so that you can then pitch this to other publishers or self-publish)?

- Who owns the rights to any expansions, different versions, and any spin-offs?

- Will your name appear on the box cover (if so, where, and what size font, etc.)?

- Will you receive a certain number of free copies of the game for yourself?

- Will you be able to purchase additional copies at cost (or at another price, and is there a limit)?

There are a number of questions you can ask and sections of the contract that can be discussed and negotiated. These are just a few items you may want to clarify.

If publishers reject your game submission, don't worry. You're going to get many more rejections than acceptances, so you have to develop a thick skin. Just because your game is rejected doesn't mean it's a bad game though. There are a number of reasons why a publisher may turn down your game, including:

- They have a game similar to yours already in their catalogue
- They are developing or are looking at a game that is similar to yours
- They are not currently accepting submissions
- Your game doesn't match their product line
- They don't feel they could sell your game at the price point they desire
- They may even love your game but aren't sure how to sell it as a product (I've been there before!)

Don't get discouraged. If at first you don't succeed, try, try again. Be persistent. If you truly think your game has what it takes to be successful, and you're getting feedback that verifies this, it may just be a matter of time. If you can't find the right publisher, you can always consider self-publishing, which is the topic of our next chapter.

If you're struggling to find a publisher or understand how to better pitch your game, you can also check out the Creation to Publication Program, which I run one to two times per year. Get all the details and join the waitlist at boardgamedesigncourse.com.

ACTION: If you're interested in pitching to a publisher, do some research to figure out who would be a good match and who is currently accepting submissions. Put together a good-looking sell sheet and contact potential publishers, but make sure to let them know if you're also contacting others. Have your rules and a play through video ready as well in case this is requested. Also, look for opportunities to meet publishers in person or offer to help or volunteer for them at Cons and other events.

CHAPTER 39
SELF-PUBLISHING

"A Kickstarter project isn't about you. It's about the backers. Focus your attentions outwardly onto your backers—make them feel appreciated and heard."

— Jamey Stegmaier, Kickstarter expert and creator of Scythe

Self-publishing may be an alternative you'll want to consider. Perhaps you can't find a publisher for your game. Maybe it's really different and unique. Maybe it has a theme that no one is interested in taking on. Or maybe you want to keep creative control and are willing to take on both the risks and potential benefits of doing this on your own.

CONGRATULATIONS, YOU ARE NOW A BUSINESS OWNER!

Make no mistake about it, if you self-publish a game, you are now running a business. You'll want to be really sure that this is right for you before making this jump. You'll actually end up spending way more time on the business aspects, and a lot less on actual game design.

There's a hidden risk in this, in that you may end up losing your passion for creating board games by being bogged down with all of the business responsibilities. However, if you love business, or the idea of running your own business, great! You may end up finding this very fulfilling.

You'll want to make sure to incorporate your business, using a Limited Liability Corporation (LLC) or equivalent, depending on where you live. This takes any liability off yourself directly, so that you will not be held responsible on a personal level for any financial liabilities. This method is a bit more work and has a slightly higher cost to get started, but is definitely worthwhile in the end to reduce financial risk.

Running your own side business will take up a lot of your free time. Here is just a partial list of the responsibilities you will need to take on yourself (or hire others to do) in order to successfully create and sell your game:

- Marketing

- Shipping

- Fulfillment

- Taxes

- Commissioning and paying for art, design, etc.

- Budgeting

- Project planning

- Researching and organizing manufacturing

- Customer service

- Methods

If you decide to self-publish, you have the choice of either doing this through **crowdfunding** or **directly**. Both of these methods have a lot in common, however they have a different starting point along with a few nuances. I'll discuss each method here.

CROWDFUNDING

Crowdfunding has become the new default for game designers interested in self-publishing. Why? It comes with lower risk, less capital investment, and allows you to gauge interest and demand for your game before setting out to have it manufactured. This can save a lot of time, money, and headaches.

I'll discuss crowdfunding at more length here, but there's so much to be said about this topic, it could fill a book. In fact, it has. There are a number of books on the market on this very subject. If you're thinking of crowdfunding, I want to guide you towards Jamey Stegmaier's excellent book, *A Crowdfunder's Strategy Guide*, which I own and strongly recommend you read, along with his Kickstarter Lessons Blog. At the very least, you'll definitely want to read his blog well before you run a crowdfunding campaign.

I've also launched the Crowdfunding Success Course, which takes you through all the steps of preparing for, launching, and fulfilling a crowdfunding campaign. I'll even review your campaign page and help you prepare for your launch so that you can drastically improve your chances of success. You can learn more about this course at jslack.lpages.co/crowdfunding-success-course.

WHICH PLATFORM TO USE?

There are multiple platforms that can be used for crowdfunding, each with their own rules, pros and cons, and followings. For board games however, Kickstarter has emerged as the most successful of these platforms by far. Other sites include Gamefound, Backerkit, Game On Tabletop, and Indiegogo. But since Kickstarter has provided so much success and has such a big market for board games, our focus will be on this platform (although the same ideas apply for these other platforms as well).

Also, make sure you know what the rules are for any crowdfunding platform you are considering. For example, Kickstarter uses an "all or nothing" funding system, where backers only have to pay, and creators only have to develop the product if the full funding goal is met. Other sites may use different funding mechanisms, so be aware of this.

SO, WHEN DO I MAKE MILLIONS?

Take note that there is a ton of competition for board games on Kickstarter. The number is increasing every year, and in 2021 there were 3,518 successful board game projects. Kickstarter raised just over $272 Million for board games that year, up from $241 Million the previous year and was almost twice the amount raised in 2017, just 4 years prior ($142 Million).

So, it's easy to think that you can just throw a game up on there and make it rich. But it's not that simple. It's important to note that of those games that were funded, only 2.9% (101 projects) had a wildly successful campaign (earning over $500,000). They also really skew the numbers, as this 2.9% accounted for more than half of all the funding received.

Did you know that roughly half of funded board game projects earned less than $10,000 in 2021? So, in reality, most projects that meet their funding goal do not exceed this by a large margin, and the vast majority raise less than $50,000. That may be enough to get a small print run of 1,000 or so games printed, which would be considered a success for a small publisher, however a big publisher would look at this as a huge fail.

Also keep in mind that this money is revenue, not profit. You are expected to use this funding to produce the games and get them into the hands of all of your backers. You probably also laid out money for art, graphic design, videography, prototypes, marketing, ads, and other expenses. Anything left over, if any, is profit, but hardly enough to live on. Especially when you'll be focused on delivering the goods and may only be able to run one or possibly two campaigns per year.

I felt that my first game, *Cunning Linguistics*, was better than many of the other party games on Kickstarter that were making big money, and I started to wonder if I could be next. But after a lot of research, I began to understand that a great game alone doesn't bring success. There is a lot more that goes into a successful campaign.

My design partner and I also realized exactly how much work goes into a Kickstarter project and didn't have the capacity to launch it when we originally wanted to. We had shot the video. We had created our Kickstarter page. We'd gotten quotes and had priced everything out. But we just weren't ready for this yet.

Eventually, we launched the game on Kickstarter and it didn't fund. But we learned a lot from this experience, which helped ensure that my next three campaigns funded very well.

Cunning Linguistics is now an afterthought. There didn't seem to be a market for it, so I've move on to other games.

Don't expect your first campaign to go gangbusters. It's usually best to start with a small campaign, grow your following, and have successively larger campaigns over time.

Note that some creators decide to cancel their campaign before time runs out if they know they won't fund. The reason in their eyes is that a cancelled project doesn't look as bad as a failed campaign. No one wants to be associated with a loser. Besides, a campaign could be cancelled for a number of reasons.

So, should you cancel your campaign if you know you're not going to meet your funding goal? That's really up to you. If you are still confident in your game, you will likely re-run it again at a later time regardless, taking the lessons you learned and feedback you get from your backers as well as non-backers to increase your chances next time. Make sure to get your backers involved and backing your project early when you re-launch.

COMPARE THE NUMBERS

Make sure to get quotes from at least three printing companies. That way you can compare them in terms of price, time, and quality. You can find printing companies by searching online, by talking with other designers, or by finding out who manufactured any of the games that you love. Make sure to also get an estimate of the weight, as this will impact the cost of freight shipping and direct shipping and fulfilment to customers.

Most printing companies are located in China, and these companies tend to produce higher quality products at much lower prices. However, the shipping may take time. Make sure you go with a company that has a reputation for delivering a good product on time and on budget. Frequent and clear communication will also be strong considerations.

There are many board game manufacturers out there. Some of the better known ones are Panda GM, Ad Magic, Longpack Games, Magicraft, and Gameland. You can find a long list containing many (but not all) game manufacturers in the resource section of this book.

YOU'LL NEED TIME

Remember, if you are launching a crowdfunding campaign, take your time. Don't rush this. It's better to get everything together and do it right the first time to increase your chances of funding, rather than having to run your campaign a second time.

Make no mistake about it – running a Kickstarter campaign is a LOT of work! I've run multiple campaigns now myself and they can keep you busy. Pretty much every other creator I have spoken to who has run one has also said it was MUCH more work than they expected. It can be really stressful and can take its toll on you.

If you have a full-time job, you will likely want to take some time off to manage the campaign, which can also be a challenge. At the very least, you'll want to remain in contact with and be accountable to your backers, not only during your campaign, but also afterwards. It's important to provide them with monthly updates at a minimum between the end of your campaign and when they have received their game so that they don't feel like you've just run off with their money!

You may think that once you've met your funding goal (and hopefully you did!) and your campaign ends, it's all easy from here. But remember, you now have to take all the steps to get your game finished, manufactured, shipped, and into the hands of your backers.

Every step of the way you'll need to work with multiple people. It's easy to run into delays or periods where your partners are busy with other projects and can't drop everything to work on yours. There's still lots to do, and it will take up a considerable amount of your otherwise free time. So, build in an extra cushion for every step, from finishing art to submitting and reviewing the files to creating and evaluating the physical sample to manufacturing to freight shipping to customer fulfilment.

KEYS TO AN EFFECTIVE CAMPAIGN

To be successful on Kickstarter (or any crowdfunding platform), it is crucial to **have a following.** It's not Kickstarter's responsibility to bring fans to the site. This is up to you.

You also have to really **market your game well.** We'll get into this more in a second, but suffice it to say that all the hugely successful board game campaigns have had both an existing following as well as really good marketing. These are the keys to success.

With all the competition, your game has to really stand out and be special. You have to include a **compelling, short video**, make sure your Kickstarter page is visually appealing by investing in some **art** (you don't have to have it all complete but should have a good amount), **lay the page out well**, include **clear and consistent pledge levels that show backers exactly what they will get**, and determine a **realistic, attainable funding goal**. You'll also want to have some really good **reviews** as well.

People buy based on emotions. They need to see themselves playing the game and having a great experience. Your game needs to look great, provide a good value, and you need to have a good hook to not only convince others that they should make a pledge for your game but also that they should back it now rather than wait.

Your video and campaign page should tell a story. Why are you here? Why should people back you? You need to create a compelling reason for them to give up their hard-earned money and trust you to deliver. Show them your passion and how you'll follow through.

GET PLANNING

It's really important to budget and project plan your campaign well. You should have received multiple printing quotes and know which manufacturing company you will be going with.

You will need to understand and have researched shipping and fulfillment, including shipping to other parts of the world (which can often be more expensive than you expect). Also try to find a way if possible to include custom fees and other taxes in your own cost rather than pass these on to your backers.

Know your crowdfunding platform's fees (for Kickstarter, their fee is 5% + 3% or so for their payment partner, so to be safe, you'll want to set aside 10%), and build in a contingency for lost and damaged products, and other possible issues. Anything can happen, so be prepared as best you can.

Your estimated shipping date is just that, an estimate, but you need to do your best to have your game out to backers by this date. Figure out how long you'll need to get all your art and design complete (if not already), a first prototype (don't skip this step, as you'll want to make sure everything is just right before your game is mass-produced), get your game manufactured, freight shipped to a distribution centre, and shipped to your customers. Then add two to three months in case anything takes longer than expected.

You'll also want to decide whether to include a portion of the shipping cost in your pledge levels or charge it in full. There are pros and cons to each approach. A lower pledge level may be more attractive, however, if the shipping cost for your backers is high relative to the pledge level (particularly if it is at least 50% or more of the cost of the game), this will turn some backers away.

If you are shipping worldwide, you'll also need to figure out the shipping rates for each region. Charging one standard shipping rate worldwide is a sure way to end up losing money. Don't guess at this. Shipping is usually a much higher expense than the actual manufacturing of the game, and underestimating and under charging for shipping is one of the biggest reasons a creator will end up losing money on a project.

You can use one fulfilment company for shipping worldwide or find regional partners. They will often help you to make arrangements for freight shipping your games to these fulfilment centres. Some may also be able to help you with payment of VAT and other taxes up front, so that customers don't end up being hit with any additional fees. Shipping rates vary worldwide, as do rates for every fulfilment partner, so do your research and base your costs on accurate numbers.

It's also wise to use a pledge manager, such as Gamefound, following your campaign. A pledge manager will allow you to collect shipping and taxes following the completion of your campaign, which you should figure out in advance and also make clear on your campaign page that these items will be collected in the pledge manager. Just do your research to understand what regions you need to collect taxes from (including UK and the EU, even if you live in North America) and ensure backers know they will pay these taxes following the end of the campaign.

Not only that, but a pledge manager will also allow you to collect late pledges for anyone who missed your original campaign and allow your original backers to upgrade their pledges and choose add-ons. When done right, this can lead to a 10-20% or more increase in funding. So, don't underestimate the power and helpfulness of using a pledge manager!

FIGURE OUT YOUR PRICE

You'll want to reward your backers for taking the chance on you, so try to keep your cost per game as well as your overall goal reasonably low in order to have a higher chance of successfully funding. Charging $50 for a simple card game with an overall funding goal of $50,000 is a sure way to show backers you either have no idea about pricing or that you're just in it to make money for yourself. Instead, involve backers and get their thoughts on different aspects. Again, you will make all decisions, but try to make sure they feel a part of your project.

When discussing your quote with your printing company, make sure to get a breakdown of what each component costs along with the cost per game at various quantities. This will allow you to decide on areas where you might cut back on or change components or parts in order to bring your backers a better price. Just make sure any changes don't take away from the experience.

Alternatively, you may want your game to be really high quality with all the best components, which may attract a premium price. However, this may be harder to fund until you've developed a strong reputation.

I'd also suggest offering your backers a price that will be the same or lower than retail price if you are thinking of continuing to sell this to customers after your campaign. Just don't jack up the price to something ridiculously higher and punish those who may not have been aware of your game previously. You do want to reward your backers for taking the chance on you. Otherwise, you may lose support for your future campaigns.

KEEP YOUR BACKERS INFORMED

Communication is also imperative. Make sure to keep your backers informed at all stages of the campaign and game production. Don't needlessly inundate them, but don't go to radio silence either. You may also receive a lot of questions and comments on your Kickstarter page, which you'll want to keep up with. Post updates regularly during your campaign to announce new stretch goals and other exciting news. Once your campaign ends, keep your backers updated at least once per month, letting them know where you're at in production. Even when there's not much to say, an update letting people know everything is on track is much better than making people wonder.

There have been some designers that have had such a difficult experience launching their game using Kickstarter that they have vowed to never use the platform again, or in some cases have given up on board game design altogether. This is typically due to a small but vocal minority of backers that have bashed the creator and made things really difficult. Hopefully you will never experience this, but be aware that this can occur.

Be prepared and make sure you can deliver your game on time and on budget and keep your backers informed. One of the worst things you can do is not update your backers regularly. People may start to question you or get concerned that they've put their trust into someone who won't be able to deliver.

PREP WORK

Take your time preparing your campaign. Many experienced creators suggest taking many months to put everything together, improving your message and getting feedback on your page and video as you go. As Jamey Stegmaier says, you don't have to launch tomorrow. Make sure you have everything in place before taking this next big step.

You'll also want to keep your campaign to a reasonable length. A 24 to 30 day campaign is pretty typical on Kickstarter. I wouldn't suggest going longer than this. While you may think that a longer window would produce more sales, this isn't the case, as you will start to lose any sense of urgency and your campaign will drag on.

So, you can start with a campaign of 24-30 days for your first project, and then you may try new things with future games. I'd love to see how someone with a following and great marketing would do on a shorter campaign of say seven days. This would lessen the month-long stress that many campaigns bring and build up the sense of urgency. Would this work though? I'm not sure, but it would make for an interesting experiment.

LIFE AFTER KICKSTARTER

There is a formula used for pricing board games. It states that you will want to sell your game for five times the landed cost. The landed cost includes the cost of manufacturing and freight shipping your game to your fulfilment or distribution partner. The final cost to consumers is known as the manufacturer's suggested retail price (MSRP). If you decide to sell your game in retail stores following your crowdfunding campaign, the distributor will typically pay you 40% of the MSRP and the retailer will pay them about 50% of MSRP.

It sounds like the retailer is making a killing here, but consider that they do have a lot of expenses like rent, employees, utilities, etc. Plus, there is no guarantee a game will sell, so they may end up needing to discount it and sell the game at break even or a loss.

Given all these numbers, you want to make sure there is some profit margin built-in here by using this 5X formula. This is generally how a publisher will determine the MSRP of a game but some may go as high as 6 or 7 times the landed cost.

On Kickstarter, you're only losing about 10% on fees, so you're getting around 90% of the MSRP yourself, which is significantly higher than the 40% you'd get from a distributor. This allows you to price your game lower on Kickstarter, giving people even more reason to back it now, rather than wait and have to pay a higher MSRP at a store later.

This brings me to another question. If your game funds successfully, what are you planning to do afterwards? Kickstarter will give you a good starting point, but it is just that. A starting point.

If you manage to get 1,200 backers, each expecting a copy of your game, will you pay for a print run of 1,500 games? 2,000 games? 5,000 games? It's really hard to tell what the demand will be afterwards.

It's beneficial to add a pre-order button or a link to your pledge manager on your call to action (CTA) button on your Kickstarter page just after your campaign closes, so that anyone who missed out on your game can still order it. You can then generate some additional orders before you commit to a number with your manufacturer.

Depending on how far over your goal you achieve, you may be able to put that profit into a larger print run. The more games you order, the lower the cost per game, however you don't want to end up with a garage full of games you can't sell. In this case, you'll be directly selling your additional games to retailers or directly to the public.

So, how will you sell those extra games?

Your best option is usually getting your game into distribution. This will allow retailers to purchase your game from that distributor, along with any other games in their catalogue and sell them directly to their customers.

However, this isn't always easy for a new publisher. Many distributors want to focus on established publishers and games that sell well in store, so indie creators are often shut out. But there are options, such as Bridge

Fulfillment & Distribution. Whereas many distributors will pay you up front for your games (usually 40% of the MSRP), these other partners may sell your games on commission. So, you'll get payouts on a regular basis (likely quarterly) based on how many of your games retailers purchased from them.

SELLING YOUR GAME DIRECTLY

There are a number of options available for you to sell your game to customers. You may decide to do this right off the bat, or follow one or more of these methods after running a crowdfunding campaign.

If you're jumping into business for the first time and are not that familiar with selling products, you might end up doing what is known as "hope marketing." This is where you put your game up for sale, hoping that if you build it, they will come. However, it doesn't tend to work this way. You want to avoid this approach and have a plan so that you don't end up with a garage or warehouse full of games collecting dust that you're paying to store.

If you decide to sell through a retailer, your best bet may be through **Amazon**. They will store, package, and send out your game for a fee. Your game will be seen by a lot of people searching in their online store, and they do all the work... aside from the marketing. You can arrange to freight ship your games directly to their warehouse, add your product to their site, and let them handle customer fulfillment for a fee. Make sure to check on their rates as they may vary depending on weight and location.

You still have to get people to find out about your game. This can be done through a number of channels such as having players review and rate your game on the site, word-of-mouth, paid or organic advertising, and showing your games at conventions and other events.

You may also want to consider brick-and-mortar retail stores. If you're going this route, there are tons of different stores you could approach, both independently run, and chain stores. This would involve visiting individual stores, demoing your game, and making the sale. This involves a lot of time and travel, and you'd be limited by your geographical location. This makes for a more personal touch but distribution gives a much better reach.

However, this could end up being a lot of work just to get a few games in a bunch of small stores. You may want to start locally and talk to any FLGS or board game cafés in your area.

You could also sell your game at conventions, from your own website or other online platforms such as Cool Stuff Inc. Try to figure out which approach would work best for you and your game.

You could also try a product launch. You see a lot of big companies like Apple run huge product launches that have people lining up for hours, if not days, to buy their hot new product. Of course, you don't quite have the size or money that they do, nor is there a huge profit margin on board games, but there are ways that you can still launch a product.

If you're interested in this approach, you might be interested in Jeff Walker. He's the king of product launches. He runs the *Product Launch Formula (PLF)* program and has also written a book called *Launch*, which outlines exactly how to follow this approach.

His book even includes a success story about a man named John Gallagher who created a board game related to medicinal herbs called *Wildcraft*. He has gone on to sell over 125,000 copies of the game since then (which is pretty phenomenal!), as well as grow a business around medicinal herbs. Keep in mind however, this game is very specialized, so don't necessarily expect the same results by launching your board game in this manner. Still, it may be worth looking into *Launch* if you're looking to sell directly.

OFF TO A GOOD START

Recognize that your campaign will have both ups and downs. It's really important to reach your funding goal as early as possible, to build confidence that your game will become a reality, both for the backers and yourself. Expect a flurry of activity on your first day or so, along with a lot of late pledges coming in on the final day or two of your campaign. Between these two times, you can definitely expect a huge lull. This is perfectly normal.

You will want to encourage your friends, family, and those following you to back your project as soon as it is launched. People want to get behind, and back, a winner. A lot of others may wait until the end due to the sense of urgency of ordering before the campaign closes. In between, there's not as much urgency and won't be as much interest in the project, but there are ways to keep the momentum going by blogging, getting interviewed, participating in podcasts, running contests, and interacting with the community. But rather than just pushing your project, try to add value first.

I also want to touch on **early bird funding**. Many campaigns have given a reduced price or bonuses for those who back a game early, particularly on the first or second day. While this may sound like a good reward for people helping out early on, it can really hurt getting funded by other backers. Just because they didn't see your campaign on the opening day, should they be penalized?

These early backers likely would have paid the extra five dollars or how-ever much you've discounted it anyway, so you're not only making others pay more, you're also leaving money on the table. This may turn other backers away. It may also be more difficult later on if you include add-ons, as you have different pricing structures for people who bought your base game, and it may get very confusing as to what the price will be if they include an add-on. Should they have to pay the full base price plus the add-on price? Save yourself the headache and avoid early bird pricing altogether.

TAKE THE PLEDGE

Let's talk about **pledge levels** and **stretch goals**. It should be clear to backers exactly what they are getting for their pledge amount. You also want to make sure your campaign is focused on your main product. If you're selling a board game, do you really want to dilute the message by offering mugs, t-shirts, and other novelties? This adds more products and levels of complexity you don't need. Just focus on your game.

You may want to include multiple item pledge levels as well, which will allow for people to buy more than one copy of your game for a slightly discounted price. For example, if you're selling your game for $39, you could offer three for $109, a savings of $8. This will encourage group buying, and reduce shipping fees for those overseas.

Keep the number of reward levels small, typically between three and five if possible. Make sure to include a one dollar pledge level. This allows people to support your project and keep up-to-date without a significant investment. Many of these backers will end up buying a copy of your game before the campaign ends.

You can include a standard pledge level and one for a deluxe version of your game. You'll often see 80-90% of backers or more pledge for the deluxe version, even if it is $10-20 more, so it is definitely worth looking into ways to create a deluxe version of your game with upgraded premium components or other extras.

Also, if your game is not too complicated for someone to build on their own, I strongly recommend considering a print and play (PNP) pledge level. This will allow more people to enjoy your game who maybe can't afford a physical copy or where shipping prices are high or shipping is restricted.

Finally, you'll want to include a retailer pledge level. This can either be a low level like $5 or a rate that is higher than other pledge levels (this may be preferred as it is less likely an individual backer will accidentally select this pledge level) and should act as a deposit for retail stores to order copies. You can later follow up with them after the campaign to finalize the order quantity, shipping details, etc. and send them an invoice for the remaining amount.

As well, your stretch goals should be related to your game and make it incrementally better. As you get more backers and raise more funds, you'll be able to put a little bit of the money you save by ordering larger quantities back into the game and reward your backers. Make sure that when you get quotes you understand exactly how much these extra components and stretch goals will cost you, because you don't want to be surprised later on and find out you're going to end up losing money on a campaign because of a stretch goal. Just don't overdo it with your first campaign. Keep it simple and manageable.

WHOSE MONEY IS IT ANYWAY?

After running a successful campaign, you may be tempted to launch your next game really soon. I caution you to ensure that your previous game has been completely fulfilled and all backers have received all their rewards before launching your next game. This will help instill confidence and the trust of your backers. If they've had a good experience with you, they will be more likely to support you again. However, if they're still waiting on your game, which is way overdue, they're not going to be tripping over themselves to throw more money at you.

Always remember, the money that backers have given you is not yours. Keep this in a separate bank account so you won't be tempted to use this to celebrate or for day-to-day expenses. This money has to go towards manufacturing and fulfilling the promise you made to your backers.

Until every backer has received their game and is completely satisfied, keep the mindset that this money is still theirs. Only at this point can you use this profit for yourself. How you use this money is up to you. If you think there is enough demand for your game, you may have decided to order a larger quantity in order to sell these post-Kickstarter, or do another print run afterwards. Alternatively, you may want to use this to help get your next game off the ground.

REVIEWS

Getting at least a few well-known reviewers to review your game is crucial for any of these options to be really successful, particularly for crowdfunding. They act as a testimonial for your game.

When choosing reviewers, make sure that your game matches the type of game that they enjoy and be sure to contact them well in advance, not halfway through your Kickstarter campaign. Be respectful, as they need time to properly review your game, and may already have a number in their queue.

If they agree to review your game, you'll want to send them a prototype that they can keep. Reviewers may also charge a fee for their review. While some feel that this is paying for a positive review, they are in fact doing a job, and it does take up a lot of their time. Many will have a first look at your game, and only accept payment to do a review if they feel that this will be helpful for you as well. That way, you won't be wasting your money and they won't be wasting their time on a review that won't be helpful to either of you.

The review may be done in video or written format, or both. This depends on the reviewer. You will use these reviews as a way to promote your game, but also as a way to help them find more viewers and gain popularity. Make sure to include a link to their review and website, so that people can see more of what they do. Remember, helping others in the board game community is always a great thing to do!

OUTSIDE THE BOX THINKING

While I've gone over the most common ways to self-publish your game, don't feel that you are completely limited to these options. Think outside the box and try to come up with some other ideas to get your games to a wider audience, and promotions that will cause a buzz. For instance, *Cranium* got their start at Starbucks, which led to a lot of success.

Board game cafés may also be willing to take a free copy of your game, which may lead to sales from people who try it out. They may even stock a small number of copies that customers can buy there directly.

Try taking your game to events, especially ones where people are sitting around or have to stand in a line for a while. If you have a good, short, compact game, there may be an opportunity to engage people who are waiting in line, and have them play your game. If they enjoy it and the price is right, they may buy a copy of it from you right there.

How about getting your game played on the radio or a TV show? I've seen clips of Ellen DeGeneres playing the game *Never Have I Ever* on her show. While I don't know the numbers, I'm sure this hasn't hurt their sales! Maybe there are online shows that would be interested in playing your game as well.

Keep all your options open. You are only limited by your own imagination. If you can find out where board game fans or potential customers may be, go to them and find an interesting way of engaging with them, without being pushy.

If neither the traditional publishing nor self-publishing options appeal to you, have no fear! The next chapter goes into some alternative options that may interest you.

ACTION: If you're considering self-publishing, decide what method you want to use. If using crowdfunding, make sure you also have a plan for what to do afterwards if you fund successfully. Know exactly what you're getting into, and prepare for your launch accordingly. Remember, take your time, and get everything done right, in order to avoid surprises later.

CHAPTER 40
OTHER ALTERNATIVES

"It doesn't matter which side of the fence you get off on sometimes. What matters most is getting off. You cannot make progress without making decisions."

- Jim Rohn, entrepreneur and author

Aside from traditional publishing and self-publishing, there are some other simpler, less stressful, less risky, and less costly options that are all offshoots of self-publishing. These include **Print-on-Demand** and **Print and Play (PnP)**. Alternatively, you may be creating your game for fun or may just be using this as a starting point to create more games. Let's get into the details of each of these methods.

PRINT-ON-DEMAND

It used to be that if you wanted to get your game printed, you'd be forced to pay for a large print run, typically 1,000 games or more. While most board game manufacturing companies still do have similar limits, more alternatives are showing up to allow game designers to print smaller batches, sometimes even individual copies.

The major player in the Print-on-Demand market is **The Gamecrafter**, a company I've previously mentioned. They can provide pretty much anything you need from custom boards and cards to various sizes of boxes to just about any component you can think of.

The Gamecrafter is the only place I'm aware of currently that will actually also sell your game directly from their website. They only print, put together, and ship each game individually when a customer orders a copy. This means that there is no major capital investment needed and you don't need to take on any of the risks that go along with printing a large number of copies.

In addition, The Gamecrafter also allows you to sell your game in crowdsales, which are similar to other crowdfunding campaigns, only on a smaller scale. The more people back your game during the campaign, the better the price becomes for your backers.

This can be a decent alternative if you're not interested in the work that goes into self-publishing or the time you could spend trying to get your game published. However, since this is done on an individual basis, the cost will generally be higher for customers and will result in a smaller margin for you. Your reach will also not be nearly as far, so don't expect a ton of sales.

There are other Print-on-Demand services popping up as well, including Print & Play, which is a division of Ad Magic, and Boardgames Maker. If your game is cards only, you might want to consider Drive Thru Cards and Printer Studio as well. These companies can print small runs of your game and turn them around quite quickly, but will be a much higher cost per game than larger manufacturers.

PRINT AND PLAY (PNP)

Print and Play (PnP) games are typically PDFs that people can download, print, cut up, and add components like dice and meeples to, in order to play at home. Note that this works better for smaller games that don't have a lot of parts and components, but won't work as well for big games with lot of items.

PnP can be used as an initial step to easily allow playtesters around the world to try your game and give you feedback, or to gain interest and possibly make available in advance for Kickstarter backers to try out. PnP files can also be your final end goal as well. You'd be providing a game that would likely be free for others to play. It's really up to you.

If you are going to create PnP games, make sure that they are print-ready for immediate use. Try printing and setting them up yourself, to ensure that everything is included and works as expected.

Make sure your files are well-formatted, laid out properly, and things like cards are sized correctly to be placed in sleeves if players choose. Minimize what is in your file and the components needed. The more work people have to do, the less likely they will want to play your game.

JUST FOR FUN

If you've spent a lot of time on your game, wouldn't you want to share it with the world? For many designers this is a resounding "yes." Then again, you may not be interested in getting your game published at all. And that's okay too! Ultimately it is your choice.

Perhaps your game is fun to play with friends and family, but maybe it has a theme that's not overly popular or is meant for such a small niche that it's just not salable. Creating a game just for fun can still lead to lots of enjoyment, and definitely involves less stress for you as a designer, as your end goal is all about creating a fun experience rather than trying to sell your game.

Remember, you can always come back to this and decide to pitch or self-publish it at a later time if you change your mind.

MOVE ON TO THE NEXT GAME

Maybe you've got your game finished and you are not sure what step you want to take next. Perhaps your game is sitting with a publisher and you're playing the waiting game. Or you have a bit of a lull during your Kickstarter fulfillment process. This may be a great time to move on to your next game idea.

However, I do caution you to figure out your end goal with your current game before moving on to another one. If you're not careful, you could end up with a lot of nearly finished games that will never see the light of day!

Having said that, it is quite often good to have multiple projects on the go once you get your first game under your belt. That way, if you get stuck on one or are in a period of waiting or just have some time between playtesting sessions, you can always be working on your next big idea.

If you enjoyed the process of creating a game as much as I do, you'll be thinking of creating more games and where this might take you in the future. You might even be tempted to look into doing this full-time. In the next and final chapter, we'll talk all about what the future might hold.

ACTION: Look into Print-on-Demand and PnP models, to see if these are right for you, either initially or as the end goal for your game. Making a PnP version of your game available can also be beneficial for playtesting and could be shared with Kickstarter backers, so having this ready will save you time later.

CHAPTER 41
DON'T QUIT YOUR DAY JOB... YET

"Never be afraid to try something new. Remember, amateurs built the ark. Professionals built the Titanic."

- Anonymous

So, you've finally finished creating your first board game. I hope it was an amazing experience for you! Maybe you've even signed on with a publisher, or have run a successful Kickstarter campaign. You may be tempted to look into doing this full-time. That's great! This shows you have a real passion and a knack for creating great games.

I do want you to be aware that there are very few full-time professional game designers out there and it is honestly pretty hard to make a living at this. That's not to say it can't be done, I just want to make sure you're setting yourself up for success before you make any big decisions (if you're thinking about this).

THE REALITY

When I finally finished my first game and started working on a number of others, I started dreaming about how amazing it would be to become a professional game designer. The problem was I hadn't sold a single game or run a crowdfunding campaign, so I only had expenditures and no revenue coming in.

Everything I read and everywhere I turned I kept hearing the message "don't quit your day job." I know the chances are slim of making a successful career at this, however I like to stay positive and try to think in terms of possibility, not probability (despite my stats background!). Others have done this, so it's not impossible.

I've also heard the expression "luck comes to those who work hard," and I firmly believe this. You may hear stories that make it seem like someone was an overnight success, but you haven't seen the countless hours, and all the blood, sweat, and tears that they've put into every moment leading up to that point. I know that if you work hard and consistently at something, you can make your dreams come true. It's all about taking the right approach.

Designing board games is amazing! It's still a lot of work and takes time, but the reward of seeing people enjoy your game and have a great experience is fantastic.

As I mentioned, very few designers are able to do this full-time. Obviously, things cost money and there is an overwhelming pressure for all of us to pay our bills. So, most board game designers do this part-time, and may be able to make a little bit of side money from it. Unless your game becomes wildly successful though, there truly is only a small amount of money to be made, and it's paid sporadically, which can make it hard to budget.

If you manage to publish one of your games, you'll receive a royalty check from time to time, but these could be few and far between. If you fulfill a Kickstarter campaign, you'll get paid within 2-3 weeks of your campaign closing, but you really need to wait until everyone has received their game before any money will go into your pocket. You may also choose to take that money and re-invest it, either in another print run of your game, or towards your next game.

Very few games are really huge successes. You can think about games and game designers in the same sphere as actors, musicians, and athletes. There are a few that are rich and famous, along with tens of thousands who you've never heard of, who are just trying to get by and make a living. That's not to say you can't do it, I'm just trying to put this in perspective.

Also, don't assume that the life of a board game designer is necessarily glamorous. They work hard. They have to constantly be coming up with new and innovative ideas, testing the heck out of them, throwing away things that don't work, and fighting to get noticed by publishers or get enough funding for their latest Kickstarter campaign. All this while more and more competitors enter the industry.

There can often be a lot of travel involved as well. Designers spend a lot of time going to conventions, playtests, and prototyping events. This can be draining, and it takes you away from your family and loved ones. Relationships may suffer as a result. If you're doing this as a business, you are also taking on all the responsibilities of the business owner, which for some is thrilling, and for others may be overwhelming.

I dabbled in game design on the side for about 4 and a half years before making the jump to full time but I did start to take it more seriously in those last couple of years. I've now been full-time in the industry for over 4 years. I have 6 games and one expansion published in those last 4 years.

I quit my day job just before I signed two of my games with different publishers. I was also very fortunate to land a contract to teach game design and development at Laurier University for a semester right around this time. However, my choice to go full-time wasn't without sacrifice.

I left a high-paying job to follow my passion and do what I wanted to do. It was only through carefully saving up, paying off all our debts, and having the incredible support of my wife that I was able to make this transition. I know that I am very privileged and lucky to be able to do this and I am very grateful for the opportunity. Few people are in the position to be able to make the jump like this.

But game design isn't all I do. I realized that diversifying and trying different things would help me to make a living in the board game industry. I now design games, publish games (self-publishing some of my own), write blogs and books on game design, and teach game design through my courses.

Even though the odds are against you, if this is your passion, then continue to follow your dream. I don't suggest quitting your day job tomorrow, but if you're good at what you do and really enjoy this, keep working at it, and one day you could be designing games full-time and doing what you really love to do for a living.

COMPETITION

As I mentioned, there's a ton of competition in the gaming world. While board game designers themselves are very collaborative and supportive of one another, publishers need to make money in order to stay alive.

I recommend concentrating on making really good games and spending time learning from others. You want your games to be amazing and really stand out!

CHALLENGES AND HOW TO OVERCOME THEM

Let's be honest. The odds of getting your game published by a traditional publisher are very low. However, you can improve these odds by targeting the right publisher for your game, and making sure your game fits well with other games in their catalogue while not being in direct competition with them.

Develop good relationships with publishers and figure out exactly what they're looking for. Maybe you have a game idea in mind you haven't developed yet and their interest in such a game will spark you to create something that's exactly what they're in the market for. If you know what they want, you can be the first one to deliver!

Remember also that Kickstarter success does not necessarily mean profit. Many designers and inventors have lost money or failed to even produce a product. Do your homework, set out a project plan, and budget well. Make sure to take unexpected costs or issues into account. Also, make sure to set a low but realistic funding goal in order to increase your chances of success.

With growing competition, you need to find a way to stand out. Make your game unique and memorable. Build a following and an audience. Give value. Make yourself an expert or go-to person in a particular area. People love to follow someone who is confident and knowledgeable.

There may not be a lot of money to be made in designing board games, however, if you build your reputation over time, you will see your audience and game sales grow!

FINAL WORDS

With each game you create, you will become a better board game designer. If your first game goes nowhere, that's ok. Your next game will be better. And the one after that will be even better.

I wish you all the success in the world and hope to play your games soon (notice I said games, and not game - if you're a game designer, your first design will definitely not be your last!).

In the meantime…

Keep learning.

Keep playtesting.

Keep designing amazing games.

ACTION: Check out the resources section for more helpful information, and be sure to download my 10 Minute Board Game Design Blueprint (bit.ly/bgblueprint) to help you move your game forward faster!

THANK YOU FOR READING MY BOOK!

I'd really appreciate your feedback, and I'd love to hear what you have to say and how my book helped you in your board game design process.

Please leave me a helpful REVIEW on Amazon.

Help me spread the word to help other designers make amazing games that we can all enjoy!

Thanks so much!

~Joe Slack

GLOSSARY OF TERMS

AP: Analysis Paralysis. Having so many choices, or such difficult choices to make, that it causes a person to not be able to make a decision.

Art vs. Graphic Design: Art refers to the visual images used in a game, as well as on the box, rulebook, and other components of the game. Graphic design relates more to the layout, formatting, and display of the game and its components. Quite often, different individuals will be responsible for the art and graphic design of a game.

Boardgamegeek (BGG): This is probably **the** site for board games and board game fans. It has ratings and reviews for pretty much every board game in existence, along with details of publishers, designers, and pretty much anything else you can think of related to board games. Here you can view the rankings of different games and see which ones are the most popular at the time.

Complexity: All games come with a different level of complexity or difficulty. In the gaming world, this is referred to as the "weight" of a game. Boardgamegeek uses a scale of 1 to 5 to rank a game's complexity (as voted on by players), where one is a very "light," easy game, with very little strategy, and five is a very challenging and strategic game (also known as a "heavy" game).

Dice Types: If you've ever played Dungeons & Dragons (or a variety of other dice-based games), you'll know that dice can come in many shapes and sizes. In the gaming world, a standard 6-sided die is known as a d6. A four-sided die is known as a d4. And so on. If you were told to roll three 8-sided dice, this would be represented by 3d8.

FLGS: Friendly Local Game Store. This is the place you'll likely go to check out new and interesting games for sale. They may even offer an area for you to try and demo games from their board game library. You'll want to find all the FLGS's in your area, as you'll likely be spending quite a bit of time there.

Iconography: The icons and images used in games to communicate information to players.

Mechanics: There are lots of things you can do in board games, actions you can take, and many different ways that things work. These are known as the **mechanics** of the game. There are lots of existing mechanics, and more being created by game designers all the time, in combination with each other, or as distinct mechanics. For a great list of mechanics and how they work, check out: https://boardgamegeek.com/browse/boardgamemechanic

MVP: Minimum Viable Product. In the case of game design, the most rough and basic version of a game that you can begin to playtest.

Playtesting: Playtesting is the act of trying out a game in development, with the goal of improving the gameplay. This can be done in different ways, and with different groups, and is a vital component of game design. Playtesting is crucial in order to find out if your game works, if it is fun and engaging, and if it achieves the experience you set out to create for players.

Point Salad: A game where there are many paths to victory and many ways to gather points. A good example of this is the game Orleans.

Reviews: Reviews are an important aspect of any finished game. These give credibility to a game and allow potential customers to understand whether this would be one they might enjoy. There are numerous established reviewers who evaluate games using video, podcasts, and/or written reviews, along with many amateur reviewers found online.

Theme: This may be self-explanatory, but is an important aspect to understand and apply to your game. Is your game about pirates? Ninjas? Zombies? Unless it is an abstract game, like Checkers or Chess, you will likely want to have a theme attached to your game, and more importantly, one that relates well to gameplay. When the theme doesn't really match the game, or seems to have been slapped on it with little thought, it is often referred to as "pasted-on."

SOME POPULAR TYPES OF GAMES INCLUDE (AND NOTE THAT THESE CATEGORIES CAN OVERLAP):

Ameritrash Games: Although it sounds derogatory, it is generally not taken this way. These games are American-style with well-developed themes and lots of player interaction. They typically have some element of luck involved. Examples: Axis & Allies, Arkham Horror.

Co-operative Games: Games in which players work together rather than competitively in order to reach a common goal. Examples: Pandemic, Burgle Bros.

Dexterity Games: Games typically involving stacking, moving, or flicking objects. Examples: Jenga, Ice Cool.

Euro Games: Also known as German or designer games, these are typically a "heavier" game with little player interaction or theme, and are based on strategy, with little luck involved. Many use worker placement mechanics, have multiple paths to victory, and have a fairly long play time. Examples: Through the Ages, Scythe.

Family Games: Game that are suitable for both adults and children. These typically have a high level of luck in order to level the playing field for kids. Examples: Monopoly, Candy Land.

Filler Game: A game that typically takes 20 minutes or less to play. These are often played as "warm up" games or in between longer games to break up the time. Examples: For Sale, Red7.

Legacy Games: These games involve multiple plays by the same group as part of a "campaign." They may involve tearing up cards, placing stickers on the board, and revealing certain things throughout the campaign. They can typically only be played once all the way through. Examples: Risk Legacy, Pandemic Legacy.

Micro Games: Games with a small footprint that are typically portable and can be played where little space is available. Examples: Love Letter, Eight Minute Empire.

Party Games: Games that involve a high level of interaction. These can be individual or team-based and are often more centred on having fun than winning. Examples: Codenames, Cards against Humanity.

Role Playing Games (RPGs): These are often played with pencil and paper, and typically involve battles and adventures. Often there is a "Dungeon Master" or similar role overseeing the campaign or adventure. Examples: Dungeons & Dragons (D&D), Tales of the Arabian Nights.

Social Deduction Games: Games in which players are trying to deduce information about other players. These often involve lots of bluffing and accusations. Examples: Resistance, Coup.

OTHER GAMEPLAY TERMS:

It is also important to distinguish what we are referring to when we say **action, turn,** and **round**.

Action: An action is a move or act that a player makes as part of their turn. Depending on the game, a player may be allowed to take one or more actions on their turn.

Turn: A turn usually consists of the action or actions that a player can take before the next player has the opportunity to take their action or actions (i.e., John is done; it's now Sarah's turn). In some games, players take their turns simultaneously.

Round: A round typically consists of all players completing their turns.

REFERENCES AND SUGGESTED RESOURCES

BOOKS

Allen, David. *Getting Things Done*. Penguin Books, 2015.

Garfield, Richard and Steve Jackson. *Kobold Guide to Board Game Design*. Open Design LLC, 2011.

Koster, Raph. *Theory of Fun for Game Design*. O'Reilly Media, 2013.

Pressfield, Stephen. *The War of Art*. Black Irish Entertainment, 2012.

Schell, Jesse. *The Art of Game Design: A Book of Lenses*. CRC PRESS, 2017.

Stegmaier, Jamey. *A Crowdfunder's Strategy Guide: Build a Better Business by Building Community*. Berrett-Koehler Publishers, 2015.

Tinsman, Brian, et al. *The Game Inventor's Guidebook*. Morgan James Publishing, 2008.

Walker, Jeff. *Launch*. Morgan James Publishing, 2014.

League of Game Makers Book Recommendations:

http://www.leagueofgamemakers.com/a-game-designers-library-14-books-you-should-read/

BLOGS, PODCASTS & WEBSITES

Board Game Design Lab – An excellent resource for information and my personal favourite podcast on game design:
http://www.boardgamedesignlab.com/

Board Game Mechanics List:
https://boardgamegeek.com/browse/boardgamemechanic

Boardgamegeek:
www.boardgamegeek.com

Cardboard Edison – website and Compendium, a great source listing hundreds of publishers:
http://cardboardedison.com/

http://cardboardedison.com/directoryinfo/

Crowdfunding Nerds
https://crowdfundingnerds.com/

Design Tips from Geek & Sundry:
https://geekandsundry.com/6-must-know-game-design-tips-from-the-creative-director-of-fluxx/

Designing for Colour Blindness:
http://blog.usabilla.com/how-to-design-for-color-blindness/

Dice Tower Game Design videos:
https://www.youtube.com/watch?v=gqqYxa3vTnU

https://www.youtube.com/watch?v=3QF2vp19PrQ

Funding the Dream – A podcast series by Richard Bliss:
https://www.buzzsprout.com/4646

Gamecrafter:
https://www.thegamecrafter.com/

Google+ Board Game Group:
https://plus.google.com/communities/111229977945579240171

How to Become a Published Board Game Designer:
https://gamedevelopment.tutsplus.com/articles/how-to-become-a-published-board-game-designer--cms-20815

ICO Partners Kickstarter Stats:
https://medium.com/icopartners/kickstarter-in-2021-for-games-6694a7c826dc

Indie Game Alliance:
https://www.indiegamealliance.com/

Inspiration to Publication (Bamboozle Brothers):
https://inspirationtopublication.wordpress.com/the-steps-for-board-games/

Kickstarter Lessons and amazing Self-publishing and Board Game Design Tips from Jamey Stegmaier of Stonemaier Games:
https://stonemaiergames.com/kickstarter/how-to-design-a-tabletop-game/

Ludology
https://ludology.libsyn.com/

Tom Vasel's Two part series on Advice to Game Designer's:
https://boardgamegeek.com/thread/107851/advice-game-designer-part-1

https://boardgamegeek.com/thread/108459/advice-game-designer-part-2

INTELLECTUAL PROPERTY

Government of Canada – Canadian Intellectual Property Office:
http://www.ic.gc.ca/eic/site/cipointernet-internetopic.nsf/eng/wr03585.html?Open&wt_src=cipo-ip-main

OTHER RESOURCES (DESIGN PROGRAMS):

Canva: https://www.canva.com/

Inkscape: https://inkscape.org/en/

GIMP: https://www.gimp.org/

Nandeck: https://www.nandeck.com/

A PARTIAL LIST OF BOARD GAME PUBLISHERS

NAME	WEBSITE
Alderac Entertainment Group	https://www.alderac.com/
Alley Cat Games	https://www.alleycatgames.com/
Amigo Games	https://www.amigo.games/
Analog Game Studios	https://analoggamestudios.com/
Ape Games	http://www.apegames.com/
Arcane Wonders	https://www.arcanewonders.com/
Asmodee	https://www.asmodee.us/en/
Atlas Games	http://www.atlas-games.com/
Bezier Games	http://beziergames.com/
Bicycle	https://bicyclecards.com/
Big Potato Games	https://bigpotato.co.uk/
Blue Orange Games	https://www.blueorangegames.com/
Board & Dice	https://boardanddice.com/
Board Game Tables	https://www.boardgametables.com/
Breaking Games	https://breakinggames.com
Buttonshy Games	https://buttonshygames.com/
Calliope Games	https://calliopegames.com/
Capstone Games	https://capstone-games.com/
CMON	https://www.cmon.com/
CMYK	https://www.cmyk.games/
Columbia Games	http://columbiagames.com
Crafty Games	https://www.crafty-games.com/
Czech Games Edition	http://czechgames.com/en/
Days of Wonder	https://www.daysofwonder.com/en/
Deep Print Games	https://deep-print-games.com/
Eagle-Gryphon	https://www.eaglegames.net/

Escape Velocity Games	http://www.escapevelocitygames.com/
Fantasy Flight Games	https://www.fantasyflightgames.com
Fireside Games	https://firesidegames.com/
Flatout Games	https://www.flatout.games/
Floodgate Games	http://floodgategames.com/
Flying Buffalo	http://www.flyingbuffalo.com/
Foxtrot Games	http://foxtrotgames.com/
Game Works	http://www.gameworks.ch/
Gamewright	http://www.gamewright.com/
Gigamic	https://en.gigamic.com/
Goliath Games	https://www.goliathgames.us/
Gozer Games	http://www.gozergames.com/
Grand Gamer's Guild	https://grandgamersguild.com/
Gravitation Games	https://gravitation.games/
Greater Than Games	https://greaterthangames.com/
Greenbrier Games	http://www.greenbriergames.com/
Grey Fox Games	https://greyfoxgames.com/
Gut Bustin' Games	http://www.gutbustingames.com/
Hans im Glück Verlags-GmbH	https://www.hans-im-glueck.de/
Hasbro	https://shop.hasbro.com/en-ca
Iello	https://iello.fr/
Imagination Games	http://www.imaginationgames.com.au/
Indie Boards & Cards	http://www.indieboardsandcards.com
Inside Up Games	https://insideupgames.com/
Keymaster Games	https://keymastergames.com/en-ca
Kid's Table Board Gaming/Burnt Island	https://www.kidstablebg.com/
Kosmos	https://kosmos.games/
Lookout Spiele	https://lookout-spiele.de/en/news.php
Magic Meeple Games	https://magicmeeplegames.com/

Matagot	https://www.matagot.com/
Mondo Games	https://mondoshop.com/
Nauvoo Games	http://www.nauvoogames.com/
North Star Games	http://www.northstargames.com/
Office Dog Games	https://www.asmodeena.com/en/
Paizo	http://paizo.com/
Pegasus Spiele	https://pegasus.de/en/
Pressman	http://www.pressmantoy.com
Ravensburger	https://www.ravensburger.us/
R&R Games	http://rnrgames.com
Renegade Game Studios	http://www.renegadegamestudios.com
Repos Production	https://www.rprod.com/en
Rio Grande Games	http://riograndegames.com/
Schmidt Spiele	https://www.schmidtspiele.de/home.html
Side Room Games	https://www.sideroomgames.com/
Smirk and Dagger	http://www.smirkanddagger.com/
Space Cowboys	https://www.spacecowboys.fr/
Spin Master	https://www.spinmaster.com/
Steve Jackson Games	http://www.sjgames.com/
Stonemaier Games	https://stonemaiergames.com/
Super Meeple	https://www.supermeeple.com/
Tabletop Tycoon	https://www.tabletoptycoon.com/
Talon Strikes Games	https://talonstrikes.games/
Talon Games	http://www.talon-games.com/
Tenzii	https://ilovetenzi.com/
The Op	https://theop.games/
Thinkfun	https://www.thinkfun.com/
Travel Buddy Games	https://www.travelbuddygames.com/
Ultra Pro Games	https://www.ultraprogames.com/
Underdog Games	https://www.underdoggames.com/
Van Ryder Games	https://www.vanrydergames.com/
Weird Giraffe Games	https://weird-giraffe-games.square.site/

Winning Moves	http://winning-moves.com
Wise Wizard Games	https://www.wisewizardgames.com/
Wizards of the Coast	http://company.wizards.com/
Wizkids	https://wizkids.com/
XV Games	https://www.xvgames.it/en/
XYZ Game Labs	https://xyzgamelabs.com/
Z-man Games	http://www.zmangames.com

Note: Make sure to check each publisher's website to see if they are currently accepting submissions, what types of games they are interested in, and their preferred submission method before contacting them.

ACKNOWLEDGMENTS

There were so many people who had a hand in this book, and I hope I haven't forgotten anyone!

Thank you so much Jamey Stegmaier, for your support, kind words, and inspirational foreword.

To all the amazing game designers and community members I've learned from, and in many cases become friends with, over the years, I couldn't have done this without learning from all of you. Thank you Chris Chung, Gabe Barrett, Rob Daviau, Steve Jackson, Matt Leacock, Sen-Foong Lim, Uwe Rosenberg, Kristian Amundsen Ostby, Vlaada Chvatil, Bruno Cathala, Michael Kiesling, Elizabeth Hargrave, Tom Vasel, Luke Laurie, Eduardo Baraf, Daryl Andrews, Sylvain Plante, Colby Dauch, Ben Gerber, Gil Hova, Daniel Zayas, Seth Jaffee, James Mathe, Artem Safarov, Mark Kolb, Pam Walls, Shannon McDowell, Ben Bratzel, Matthew Hester, Kevin Carmichael, Allysha Tulk, Peter Hayward, Daniel Rocchi, Harry Timson, Raf Rahman, David Van Drunen, Jeff Fraser, Andy Kim, Damian Fleming, Maddox Campbell, Rod Currie, Stefano Liseno, and Mitchell Allen.

Thank you to my editor, Rebecca Reid, who made my book so much better.

Thank you to Drew Corkill for the amazing job you did formatting the book!

Thanks to Mitch Morris for designing the excellent cover.

A huge thanks to Shawn Clouthier, who read my early manuscript and provided invaluable input. You made The Board Game Designer's Guide even more helpful!

Thanks to my writing coach, Scott Allan, and the wonderful Self-Publishing School community.

To my oldest friend (what are you, a hundred now?) Jason Deline, for all your help with the audio book and your undying support.

To my great friends and family, Matthew Guillemette, Margie Guillemette, Miles Bossons, Aizick Grimann, Lubin Martinez, Lucas Cesarone, Daniel Longmire, Dave Neal, Renee Laviolette, Matt Mitchell, Cory Bildfell, Rob Slack, Kerri Beaulieu, Penny Slack, John Acuna, Cindy Alexander, Helena Patte, Caitlin Hartley, Jordan Loshinsky, Melissa McCarthy, Kate McDougall, Stu Sackler, Siva Bradshaw, Shannon Boyce, Marco Garcia, Todd Taylor, Helen Deline, Gary Deline, Paul Brown, Nan Brooks, Jane Goldthorpe, Mike Sone, Adam DeVita, Frances Maxwell, Voula Maroulis, Jeremy Banks, Chris Cormier, AJ Brandon, Nathan Frias, Chad Nikolic, Margarita Prunskus, Pat Prunskus, Yvonne Tellis, James Pawelkiewicz, Leah Smith, Adam Smith, Momo MacLeod, Dave Rossi, Belinda Rossi, Krista Miller, Bernard Blassnig, Rob Routh, Kim Routh, Anna Murray, Helen Taylor, Steve Camacho, Andrew Gibson, Deb Piskunov, and Maks Piskunov. Thank you all for your support and playing so many early prototypes of my games.

Thank you to my parents, Nancy and Bob Slack. Thank you for everything you do and for always being so supportive.

Last but not least, thank you Lisa and Evan, for putting up with me, especially all the time that I put into this book and designing board games. You are the best! I couldn't have done this without you.

ABOUT THE AUTHOR

Joe Slack is a healthcare data guru turned board game designer. He has now combined his passions for board game design and helping others into one. That means he works with other board game designers to help them get unstuck and create amazing games they will be proud to share with the world.

Joe is a board game designer, publisher, instructor, and the author of the **#1 international best-selling book, The Board Game Designer's Guide**, along with 3 other books on game design. He has **taught Game Design and Development at Wilfrid Laurier University** and runs the **Board Game Design Course**, an online course for new game designers, in addition to courses on getting published and running a successful crowdfunding campaign.

Joe has **4 games published** with other publishers (Zoo Year's Eve, Kingdom's Candy: Monsters, Four Word Thinking, and King of Indecision) and has successfully crowdfunded and self-published multiples games including 14 Frantic Minutes, Relics of Rajavihara and the expansion Montalo's Revenge.

Check out his website https://www.boardgamedesigncourse.com/ for more resources and information on his books and courses.